J. Winston

Cora O'Kane

Or the Doom of the Rebel Guard - A Story of the Great Rebellion

J. Winston

Cora O'Kane
Or the Doom of the Rebel Guard - A Story of the Great Rebellion

ISBN/EAN: 9783337213183

Printed in Europe, USA, Canada, Australia, Japan

Cover: Foto ©ninafisch / pixelio.de

More available books at **www.hansebooks.com**

CORA O'KANE;

OR,

THE DOOM OF THE REBEL GUARD.

A Story of the Great Rebellion.

CONTAINING

INCIDENTS OF THE CAMPAIGN IN MISSOURI UNDER GENERALS FREMONT AND SIGEL, AND THE THRILLING EXPLOITS OF THE UNIONISTS UNDER MAJOR ZAGONYI.

By SERGT. J. WINSTON.

PUBLISHED BY AN ASSOCIATION OF DISABLED SOLDIERS.

1868.

CORA O'KANE;

OR,

THE DOOM OF THE REBEL GUARD.

CHAPTER I.

THE last month of the year 1860 will long be remembered by the people of this generation, and will be marked as a great epoch in history in all coming time. The causes that produced the seeds which at last ripened into outward strife, it is not our purpose to dwell upon. It is not within our province so to do. We are not writing a history, but simply relating a story of every-day life that occurred where passion and animosity reigned in the hearts of men, arising from imaginary grievances which brought misery and ruin to many firesides that were but a little while before so peaceful and happy; and all this will be seen by the reader as he peruses the following pages.

In the early part of the spring, 1861, in the small town of Osceola, on the Osage River, in Missouri, stood a house of magnificent appearance for that remote part of the country, which but a little before was a howling wilderness. Its style of architecture was wholly confined to the taste of the occupant. Its lower rooms were large and airy, and with its huge chimneys, built upon the outside, besmeared with smoke as they were, with a very little imagination might be conjured into the turrets and towers of a baronial castle — especially when viewed from a distance. The building fronted the river, and from its front door, with its ivy-woven stoop, led a commodious walk to the water's edge. The kitchen and the apartments prepared for the servants were si

ated in the rear part of the structure. North of the house stood
the cottage of the overseer, with outhouses and sheds, while off
in the same direction might be seen the habitations of the field
hands, that were very neatly arranged into streets. East and west
from the buildings, extending back from the river, stretched the
broad plantation, containing many acres. There was no other
dwelling in the immediate neighborhood. It was more than two
miles to the residence of the next planter, whom we shall call the
Hon. John McBride; and, owing to his astonishing influence over
the planters in Osceola and vicinity, it became the hotbed of Secession. It is true that it was also the residence of some of the most
devoted and self-sacrificing Union men which the country produced
in that trying time; yet by far the greater part of its inhabitants
warmly espoused the cause of Secession.

For some time previous to the commencement of our tale, the
Gulf States had been agitated by their leading minds with the
pernicious doctrine of State Rights, and in Missouri it found many
advocates, where the continual discussion of this question caused
party feeling to run high. Families were divided upon the great
question, and in many instances they were completely broken up
and separated—so tenaciously did each cling to their opinions. And
now, that ten of the states were determined to array themselves
against the government, emissaries were sent into this state to
strengthen their cause, and their aggravating conduct had engen-
dered a feeling of deep and bitter hostility between the inhabitants
of this section, which only waited to display itself in deeds of violence and cruelty when a fitting opportunity should occur.

The house described to the reader was the residence of Thomas
O'Kane, a wealthy and influential man, who had now become one
of the most unrelenting and determined leaders of Secession in this
part of the country. He held a commission from the state government as a magistrate, and was now appointed colonel by the
Confederate authorities; and he unscrupulously and unsparingly
used his authority to the advancement of the Confederate cause,
and to the injury and oppression of the few Union men who lived
within the reach of his influence or power. He was a middle-aged
man, somewhat above the ordinary size, with dark, repulsive features, and an eye that glanced constantly with sinister expressions.
He was a widower, his wife having died a few years previous to his

introduction to the reader, leaving him only one child, a son, who was absent from home for the purpose of receiving an education. Since the death of his wife his household affairs had been under the management of his wife's sister, a sallow, dried, and withered maiden of some forty years, who was every way as tyrannical and overbearing, and, withal, as warm a Secessionist, as her brother-i.-law. Both were feared and reverenced by their Secession neighbors, and both were heartily detested by the Unionists within the circle of their acquaintance.

Up to the time of which we are now writing, the Unionists and Secessionists of this vicinity had not come to any open and serious rupture. The mutually exposed and accessible situation of their property had, in a great measure, tended to restrain the violent passions that were burning in their breasts, for they feared the injuries which each might do the other, and they well knew that, under the existing state of affairs, these injuries would be irreparable. But it was evident to all that the plot was thickening, and the time was not far distant when the mutterings and threatenings of the storm must be exchanged for the storm itself.

In addition to the sister-in-law above mentioned, the family of O'Kane consisted of a niece, the daughter of a deceased brother, who had died in New Orleans of a prevailing epidemic. He left an immense fortune, which he bequeathed to this daughter and her heirs, if she left issue; but in case she died childless, the whole should revert to O'Kane and his heirs. The uncle was made guardian to his niece, and executor of the last will and testament of the deceased. Cora O'Kane was scarcely seventeen, yet she possessed remarkable beauty. She was above the ordinary size, and her form, although not gross, was large and voluptuous. Her countenance owed not its attractions so much to symmetrical "rule and compass" dimensions and proportions, as it did to the peculiar and winning expression which it wore. Her eye, a dark hazel, could express every passion, from the tenderest emotions of the soul to the wildest bursts of enthusiasm and resentment. Her hair was dark and glossy, and she usually wore it destitute of curls or ornament, and in such a manner as developed the beautiful and classical proportions of her head. In early infancy she had lost her mother, yet her father had spared no pains or expense in the culture and training of her mind.

Cora had been a resident of the house of her uncle some three years previous to 1860, and although her situation, destitute of father and mother, was such as would readily command the sympathy of almost any individual, yet she had experienced but sorry treatment at the hands of her guardian and the "withered crone" she was obliged to call *aunt*. She well knew the cause of this treatment, for, young as she was, she possessed sufficient penetration to read the character of her uncle; and she knew that his whole life was bound up in political distinction and the acquirement of wealth. She knew, also, although nothing had been said to her directly upon the subject, that it was the intention of her uncle to wed her to his son, — who was at this time absent, receiving his education, — thereby securing to his own family the estate which she possessed; but, in her own mind, she had determined to die rather than consent to the union. She always undisguisedly manifested an aversion for him, and she well knew that such conduct chagrined and mortified the uncle and aunt. She was also a warm Unionist. Her whole soul was enlisted in the cause of the loyal people, and she sought not to disguise this fact from her uncle. These causes, she justly concluded, led the uncle to treat her with severity.

Her cousin, William O'Kane, whose amorous addresses she had rejected, was a tall, ill-formed youth of some twenty years, with coarse, repulsive features, and in disposition equally as overbearing as his father. He was strongly conceited in favor of his own person and understanding, and seemed, in fact, to regard himself as the embodiment of all that was beautiful and desirable. His political opinions were the same as his father's; and, indeed, the astonishing ingenuity which he displayed in insulting and tormenting his Union neighbors was the very circumstance that had induced his father to send him away to be educated. He was utterly incapacitated naturally from forming an attachment which could call forth any of the finer and nobler feelings of man's nature; yet he had been heard to say that his cousin Cora "was tolerably good looking, and as rich as Cæsar." Undoubtedly the youth imagined this, coming as it did from his noble self, as a compliment of no trifling importance, and as one that was to commend him especially to the young lady concerning whom it had been spoken. When he was last at home, his father had disclosed to him his intentions in relation to his union with Cora, and he was instructed to report himself at home at the next vacation in order that the nuptials might be celebrated. Accustomed to an unlimited control in all things, he did not deem it of the least importance to consult his niece upon a matter which involved so vital and important an interest of hers.

During the spring of 1861, Thomas O'Kane, in connection with John McBride and other Secession leaders, was employed in arranging and disposing of plans for the prosecution of the war, which, it was now obvious to the commonest understanding, would shortly be upon them. The Unionists of this vicinity were not idle in the mean time. As we have before stated, they were few in number; but in determination and enthusiasm they were a host. They held frequent meetings in private and secluded places, being determined to establish as good and effective an organization as the circumstances of the case would allow.

About half way between Osceola and Warsaw, and but a few rods from the banks of the Osage, was the cabin of a young hunter, who was known among the settlers by the name of Marvin Wilson. He first came into this region some three years previous to the opening of this narrative; and although his language, his bearing, and indeed his whole appearance, denoted that he had been highly educated, and reared in the first society, yet he proceeded to erect a cabin for himself in a secluded spot, and immediately after assumed the guise of a hunter — pursuing any and all game whose fur was in the least degree valuable. He was tall, nobly proportioned, with a countenance and aspect that at once convinced the beholder that he was no ordinary individual. His eye was large and piercing, his forehead high and ample, and his raven hair hung in long, glossy ringlets around a neck that might have furnished a painter with a model. There was nothing aristocratic or overbearing in his action or language, yet he seemed formed to lead, and all who came into his presence felt that they were willing to obey. He dressed, in pursuance of his vocation, in a kind of semi-military style, and his rifle was his never-failing attendant. All in all, he was as noble and elegant a specimen of manhood as eye could wish to gaze upon.

His cabin was built at the base of a rocky eminence that rose abruptly from the shores of the river, and was composed in part of logs, and partly of the hill itself, which had been excavated for that purpose, afterwards lined securely with logs, roughly squared with an axe, and covered with the skins of deer and other animals. A small door, one part of which served also as a window, afforded ingress and egress, and just above the bark roof of the wooden part of the edifice passed a rough stone chimney. His furniture consisted of two rough-made stools, a bench, or table, to match, a small Indian looking-glass, a kettle, and one or two coarse culinary utensils. His bed, which was placed in the excavated portion of the cabin, was composed entirely of the skins of animals. On a shelf, that stretched nearly around the whole apartment, was a razor and comb, and a few other articles of the toilet, and just beside the door was a huge fireplace, which did infinite credit to the prevailing fashion in relation to such indispensable appurtenances.

Here, in this secluded place, Marvin Wilson had lived since his advent into this region. None knew whence he came, or what his former life had been. He was about twenty-eight years of age, which he manifested no anxiety to conceal; but when questioned in relation to his connections or former residence, his brow became gloomy, and his answers were such as caused his interrogators to desist from their scrutiny. Marvin Wilson was a strong Unionist, and he possessed a powerful and persuasive eloquence, and a keen and biting satire, which he used fearlessly upon all occasions in favor of his adopted state remaining in the Union. He was fairly adored by his Union friends, who made him their leader; and at the fall election, prior to the breaking out of the rebellion, he was elected to the legislature from his precinct, and manfully did battle for the Union cause. When he returned from the capital, in March, he found that Thomas O'Kane had taken a decided stand in favor of secession. Up to this time Marvin had been acknowledged a guest at the house of O'Kane. He was now acknowledged and allowed as such no longer. It was more than rumored that Cora O'Kane and Marvin were inexpressibly dear to each other, although from the watchfulness of the uncle it was impossible for them to enjoy anything like uninterrupted communication. Rumor or no rumor, it is certain that when the name of Cora O'Kane was mentioned, the eyes of Marvin brightened; and when Cora gazed upon him, it was with a heightened color in her cheek, and a heaving at the breast, that denoted unusual emotion.

William's vacation at last arrived, and, punctual to the requirements of his father, he returned, and all the domestics of the house were busily engaged in making preparations to celebrate the nuptials of the hopeful youth and his cousin.

CHAPTER II.

IN about a week after the announcement had been made that Marvin Wilson's presence was no longer desired at the house of O'Kane, as we have stated in the previous chapter, Cora was sitting in her room, pleasantly engaged in reading, when her uncle entered, and unceremoniously seated himself by her side. His brow was unusually open and smooth, and a famished-looking smile was struggling for a resting-place around his lips. It was plainly evident to the young lady that some enterprise was in view which her gallant uncle was intending to carry by smiles and suavity. After a short interval he turned to her.

" Cora," said he, " Cora, my child, these are uncertain and very gloomy times. We are threatened with a war, through the misconduct of a few hot-headed and deluded men, and there is no telling what its consequences may be to us. We may be ruined by it, my child."

Cora particularly noticed the endearing appellation of " my child," which, for the first time in his life, the uncle had bestowed upon her. She thought of the fable of the wolf and the lamb, but determined not to be outdone by her relative in the game he had undertaken to play.

" My *dear* uncle," she answered, "I am well aware that these are dangerous times. It seems to me that if we continue to give aid to Secession, and persist in the harsh measures of our leaders, war will inevitably be the consequence."

" No," replied the uncle, " our Confederate leaders are not in the wrong ; it is these cursed, low-born Unionists. There's where the difficulty lies."

" I am sure, uncle, the Unionists ask nothing but what is reasonable and right," replied Cora ; " their only desire is to remain in peace under the protection of the old flag, and adhere to the institutions handed down to them by their fathers."

2

The brow of O'Kane lowered, but recollecting himself, he replied, —

"Well, well, we will not discuss politics, Cora. I came to talk with you on a more pleasing theme. You are now, let me see — how old are you, Cora?"

"I am a little past seventeen," replied she.

"Yes, yes, I might have known," continued O'Kane, musingly, "I might have known; but the fact is, I am growing old and forgetful. You are now at that age when you begin to — a — want a — a — when, in short, Miss Cora, nearly all young women want a suitable companion of the opposite sex. Ha, ha, ha!" and he forced a laugh to conceal his confusion.

"I must confess, uncle," replied Cora, slightly coloring, "that I have not yet experienced the *want* of any such companion as you have set forth."

She dropped her eyes confusedly as she concluded her reply, for the image of Marvin flitted past her mind's eye.

"The *want* is not, perhaps, the proper term," continued O'Kane, who had observed the emphasis with which Cora had repeated it. "I should have said *desire*, perhaps."

"I have neither experienced desire nor want," replied Cora, intently gazing at nothing.

"You will soon be eighteen years of age," continued O'Kane, "and then, according to my brother's will, you are to enter upon the possession of your fortune. You are very young, Cora, to manage so large a sum prudently, and I had come to the conclusion to offer you a young man as a husband who would be most likely to manage your property in a way the most conducive to your happiness and enjoyment. You ought to know, Cora, that this is not with me a matter of interest, for in case you should die without heirs, the property reverts to me, or, should I be dead before you, to my heirs."

"I am willing to give you credit for perfect disinterestedness," replied Cora, "but, my dear uncle, I choose to marry whom and when I please."

O'Kane bit his lips at this announcement, and a pause of a few moments ensued. At length he resumed, in a melancholy tone, —

"You are the only child, Cora, of my only brother, and I am

sure I may be pardoned for interfering in your arrangements. My brother often wrote to me in his letters that nothing would give him so much happiness as to see our families united by the strongest ties of affinity and friendship. He's gone now, poor fellow" (here he dropped a tear), "yet, if we are aught in heaven as we are on earth, he must desire so pleasant a state of affairs. I will not conceal from you the fact that my son William loves you, and is willing and anxious to become your protector; and I will not deny that I had fondly anticipated such an event."

The allusion to her father brought the tears to the eyes of Cora, and when her uncle concluded his hypocritical speech, she was still in tears. She determined, however, to put a final end to any such anticipations as O'Kane had described, and she answered accordingly.

"I should be glad of an opportunity of accommodating my uncle, but, in this particular, I cannot. I never can be the wife of William. I love him not, and can never love him; and I beg, sir, that this may be the last time you will ever speak to me on the subject."

"I'll be d—d if you shall not have him!" exclaimed O'Kane furiously, striking his fist against a small table standing near with such violence that it fell upon the floor. "I'll be hanged if you shall not have him! Your mind has been poisoned with the infernal doctrines of the Unionists. That accursed adventurer, Wilson, would perhaps suit the fastidious taste of your ladyship better! But you are yet under my control, thank God!"

The fury of her uncle somewhat alarmed Cora; but as it was not quite unexpected, she soon recovered herself, and somewhat proudly replied, —

"Your son must rejoice in the man he has selected as his wooer. Oaths and gesticulations go far to win the heart of a timid girl!"

O'Kane saw at a glance where he had missed his calculation, but it was too late to go back. His violent passions had obtained the mastery. He therefore said, —

"Taunt me not, madam, for you cannot elude me. I have you fast, and there are none to scrutinize or ask the cause of my conduct. I tell you again that you shall wed my son or you shall never wed. I am not the man to jest. I am one who resolves and executes."

"It is not my poor person that your son covets," replied Cora; "it is my property. I feel confident that my fortune would satisfy him, and I am willing this night to convey it all, every farthing, to

him, provided his father will never again bring up to me the subject
of my union with him. Take the whole; I give it freely, rejoi-
cingly."

This annunciation cut O'Kane to the quick. He was naturally a
proud man, and when he saw that Cora had so correctly divined
the power of her attractions, he felt mortified, and, despite his lack
of shame, looked abashed. Lowering his tone materially, however,
he replied, —

"My son is not a beggar, madam; neither will he be portionless
when he arrives at his majority. This sarcasm will not materially
advantage you, you may depend upon it. My word in regard to
your union is passed. I never, *never* retract."

As he concluded speaking, he turned on his heel and quitted the
apartment, leaving Cora alone.

Her feelings may be better imagined than described. She was
completely in the power of her uncle, and she saw no way to escape
the odious union; yet she determined, at all hazards, to brave her
uncle's wrath, and, in fact, to die rather than submit to his requirements. In the midst of her perplexities the door again opened,
and her aunt entered. Seating herself in an unoccupied chair, and
pursing up her mouth to the smallest possible dimensions, she thus
addressed Cora : —

"So, miss, you have refused to accept the offer of your kind
uncle — eh? A pretty thing, truly! A young girl, like you,
refuse an offer of that kind! Things have come to a pretty pass,
indeed!"

The hag here made a slight pause, and gazed fiercely at Cora,
who sat silent and weeping. Giving her head a toss, she resumed, —

"I wonder what you can think of yourself, miss! I wonder what
plans you have concocted for your future existence! May be you
think to get a lord, or a duke, or some other great man! I declare,
if I ain't beat! Refuse Mr. William! I guess a girl of your age
in my day would never refuse such an offer as that."

In this strain Miss Rebecca (for so the aunt was called) continued to berate the poor girl until she exhausted her own breath, and
was obliged to give it up. To all her taunts, Cora replied not a
word; and when, in a short time after the conclusion of her last
endeavor, her aunt retired, she sought her bed, but not to sleep.

A hundred different plans her tortured ingenuity suggested whereby she could escape from the persecution of her uncle; but her reason rejected them all. At one time she resolved to acquaint Wilson with the whole affair; but, upon second thought, her modesty forbade it. At another time she resolved to fly from beneath her uncle's roof; then her reason asked her where she should go, and by what instrumentality escape. In this manner she lay and planned, and arranged and rearranged, until morning, when she arose feverish and unrefreshed.   She met her uncle and her cousin at the breakfast table with fear and trembling; but the meal passed off in silence, nor could she detect a ray upon the countenance of either which could afford her the slightest clew as to what conclusion her conduct of the previous night had caused them to arrive.

For several weeks she lived in constant dread of a renewal of her cousin's suit; yet she was disappointed. Not a word was spoken upon the subject by either her uncle or her cousin, and even old Rebecca had ceased to make it the groundwork of her diurnal lectures.   Cora flattered herself that the hateful match was forgotten, that her uncle had thought better of his duty and his interest, and she began to be even cheerful and comparatively happy. Nay, she even could bear the presence of Mr. William, and frequently engaged him in some of the lighter amusements of the moment. Poor girl! with all her tact, she knew not with what a monster she was dealing.

CHAPTER III.

It was not far from the middle of June that O'Kane returned home from a few days' absence. He had been raising troops for the defence of the Confederate authorities in the state. The inmates of the house gathered around him in silence as he related to them how well they had got their state guards organized, and his hopes of success. And, as Cora came down to greet him, he said very emphatically that all Lincoln's minions in Missouri must bow to the superiority of his Confederate guards.

"My dear father," said William, "inasmuch as you are to be at home for a few days, what say you for inviting our neighbors and friends, and having a sociable here?"

To this he readily assented, and the rest of the day was occupied in making preparations for the dance. The next morning, at an early hour, all was bustle around the house. The servants, with their shining black faces, were running to and fro from the kitchen to other parts of the house, while on the lawn around the house seats were prepared for the invited guests, and grinning Africans, with cracked fiddles in their hands, were waiting for the company to assemble on the lawn — which they did early in the forenoon. The exercises commenced with a spirited political harangue by Colonel O'Kane on the righteousness of the Confederate cause; after which the celebrated ballad, "Success to the Bonnie Blue Flag," was sung by the whole company, with Sambo playing the accompaniment on his cracked fiddle. The dancing now commenced, and all went merry as a marriage bell. After the dancing ceased, the company were treated to a luxurious feast that was served up to them on tables in the open air. They had not fairly commenced.feasting when the attention of the whole company was directed to a skiff which was rapidly advancing in the river from the direction of Warsaw. In her bow waved the "bonnie blue flag." As the boat neared the land, in the direction of the house, in a few moments her slight keel grated upon the pebbly shore, and three men leaped upon the sward and hastened towards the table. No sooner had they arrived within speaking distance than Colonel O'Kane addressed them.

" What news do you bring? "

After the sergeant had saluted him, he said that General Frost and his men had been surprised by six thousand Unionists under the command of Colonel Blair, and he, of course, had to surrender.

" Were you there at the time? " asked Colonel O'Kane.

" No, sir; I had been detached to the headquarters of General Price, as an orderly, and here is a note from him."

The colonel seized the note with a trembling hand, tore open the envelope, and read aloud as follows : —

" BOONVILLE, June 28.

" DEAR COLONEL : General Frost has got into a tight place, and with him are gobbled up the munitions and guns that arrived so lately from the Baton Rouge Arsenal for our use. Therefore I command you to remain in your vicinity and recruit as many men as you possibly can, and we will contrive to provide you with equipments as fast as possible. You are promoted as colonel of this special Guard, with the rank of brigadier general; and as you already retain the civil office of magistrate in your county, we give you the power to try and hang any man that dares to usurp your power or thwart you in your course.   Yours, respectfully,

"STERLING PRICE,
"*Major General of the State Forces.*"

"Then," said the colonel, folding up the letter, "I am to be the commander of a special guard, and *woe* to the man or men that will not enlist at my command and make obeisance to the bonnie blue flag. And be assured, my friends," he said, turning around to his visitors, they being all Secessionists, "this vicinity shall be cleared of these accursed free-labor men and Unionists before the next three months." Then stepping to one of the tables he seized a bottle of wine, and said, "Let us drink a bumper to the noble Guard we are going to raise."

He was here interrupted by the loud baying of two hounds in the forest, apparently but a few rods south of the house. The whole group turned their heads in the direction of the sound, and in a few moments a noble buck bounded into view, instantly followed by two dogs, all making directly for the river. It was apparent that the deer was nearly spent, yet he dashed past the group of gazers without appearing to notice them, and, clearing the fence at the lowest end of the yard, struck boldly into the river, closely pursued by the dogs.

"Whose dogs are those?" questioned O'Kane, eagerly gazing at the exciting scene.

"They are Marvin Wilson's, father," replied William. "I have often seen them follow him."

"Marvin Wilson's!" exclaimed O'Kane, anxiously turning to his son. "How came they here, I wonder?"

"Probably he's close at hand himself," responded the son. "Perhaps my cousin Cora knows if that be the case?"

All eyes were turned upon that young lady, who suddenly grew deadly pale, and both dogs and deer were forgotten.

"I know nothing at all about it," she said, faintly, seeing that she was expected to speak. "My cousin knows that I have no opportunity of being acquainted with the movements of Mr. Wilson."

"It's to be hoped that he'll follow his dogs," exclaimed O'Kane, fiercely. "I think we'll make his welcome comfortably warm — won't we boys, eh?"

" Ay, ay," responded the guests.

" Well, if you've got through talking with those men, I can't see what use there is in letting the dinner spoil for the sake of Marvin Wilson," exclaimed aunt Rebecca, in something of a rage.

" That's true, sister," replied O'Kane. "Come, my friends, let's renew our meal," he added, turning to his guests. "And here you, William, give our worthy friends from General Price something to drink, and see that they be well provided with eatables."

The whole company again seated themselves at the table, and in a short time the meal was despatched. Soon after the conclusion of the feast, the party was again assembled upon the shore to witness the embarkation of General Price's men, who were now about to return to that officer's headquarters. The boat was ready to shove off, and O'Kane was freighting the ears of the sergeant with intelligence and messages for General Price, when a slight scream from some of the junior female members of the party attracted the attention of all.

" What's the matter?" suddenly exclaimed O'Kane, partially turning round.

" See yonder, father!" said William, pointing with a trembling finger in the direction of the barns.

The whole party simultaneously gazed in the direction designated by the young man, and observed the finely-proportioned figure of Marvin Wilson slowly approaching. He was dressed in a plain green hunting-shirt, with buckskin underclothes and moccasins, with a rifle thrown carelessly across his arm. He evidently saw the group near the river, yet he steadily held on his way towards them. The countenance of O'Kane grew dark and frowning, the female portion of the company looked anxious and timid, and the whole assembly awaited his approach in silence. In a few moments the young hunter approached them, and turning to the ladies with a smile and a bow, exclaimed, —

" Good afternoon, ladies and gentlemen. Do not let me interrupt your pleasures. I would merely inquire if any of you have seen two dogs pass this way in pursuit of game?"

" Who the devil are you, that talk of interrupting our sports in this cavalier manner?" coarsely replied O'Kane. " Do you know where you are, sirrah?"

" I thought I was upon the premises of a gentleman," calmly replied Wilson, " but I see I am mistaken."

"None of your wit at the expense of me or my guests, caitiff!" retorted O'Kane. "Those who seek to imbrue their hands in the blood of their neighbors can expect courtesy from the hands of no one."

"Then *you* should take no offence at my interruption," exclaimed Wilson, slightly kindling.

"Come on; let's flog him!" fiercely cried O'Kane.

"Yes, yes," responded several of the bystanders, "that's the sort! flog the scoundrel!"

A slight groan resounded from the knot of females, and Cora O'Kane fell to the ground senseless. She was immediately raised in the arms of some of her companions, whilst others stepped to the river's brink for water. In a few moments she revived.

"You had better take Cora to the house, Rebecca," said O'Kane. "It may hurt her conscience to see a Unionist justly dealt by."

Rebecca proceeded to lead Cora towards the house, followed by all the females of the group. As the trembling girl passed Wilson, she gave him a glance that penetrated to his inmost heart. It spoke to his understanding more than volumes could reveal. As soon as the females left the ground, O'Kane again turned and addressed himself to Wilson.

"I will tell you, young sir, in order that you may know the reasons for our conduct, that we are perfectly acquainted with your character and designs. You are a base and murderous Unionist, and are this moment enga—"

"That I am a Union man I will never deny," fiercely interrupted Wilson, his eye flashing fire; "but whoever says I am base or murderous is a liar in his throat!"

O'Kane's inflamed features paled at this fierce annunciation, but, casting his eye upon the group of sturdy men by whom he was surrounded, he continued, not noticing the interruption, — "this moment engaged in a plot with another lawless marauder to murder all the Confederates in this vicinity. Can you deny this charge, villain that you are?" he added, with a malicious grin.

"How brave a coward can be when supported by bands of friends!" sneeringly replied Wilson, at the same time pointing a finger at O'Kane. "Give me but a chance for fair play," he continued, "I pledge myself to make you acknowledge what you have asserted now to be as base a lie as your black heart can conceive."

3

"Have a care what you say, villain, for you are in my power, and I could string you to the first tree in the forest if I chose. Have a care!"

"Have a care!" sneeringly responded Wilson; "another evidence of your dastardly cowardice! Threaten a man when you are surrounded with forces in abundance! I know not what you may choose to do with me, nor do I fear for the consequences; but this much I do know; one among your number is a dead man if any of you dare assault my person."

Saying this, Wilson brought his rifle aport, and was about setting back the cock, when Sergeant Hughes, who had crept behind him unperceived, threw both his arms violently around his waist, and the rifle fell to the ground. It was immediately seized by one of the bystanders, who discharged it in the air and threw it upon the grass. A violent struggle ensued between Wilson and Hughes; but the mass coming to the assistance of the sergeant, Wilson was soon overpowered and thrown upon the ground. His hands and feet were next securely bound with a strong rope, which was provided by O'Kane, and he was then left to struggle at his leisure. The Confederates speedily formed a ring around him, and stood gazing upon him with evident delight.

"What do you say to shooting folks now, you d—d scoundrel?" said Hughes, who was standing just outside the ring, half bent, while the blood ran from his nose in a stream.

"Let's make him huzza for Jeff Davis!" shouted William, gazing exultingly upon his fallen rival.

"Huzza! glorious!" shouted a dozen voices. "Make him huzza for Jeff Davis. 'Twill do his Yankee throat good, though it disgraces Davis's name."

"Let's tie him to one of the pines," cried William; "and then, my boys, we'll flog him until he huzzas."

"Glorious!" shouted the rabble; and away they ran — some for ropes, with which to secure him to the tree, and others for whips, to force him to a compliance with their wishes.

Wilson lay upon the ground during this brutal arrangement with his eyes closed. He felt it was in vain to struggle. He knew he was completely in the power of his enemies. His rage in the first instance was almost unbounded, but he gradually worked himself calm. He was possessed of strong, nay, violent, passions; yet he was a person of reason and reflection. He was utterly insensible to fear; yet when he heard them announce their determination of flogging him, an unusual sensation crossed his breast. It was not fear, yet it was a sort of disgusted dread of so degrading and unmanly a punishment. In his present situation he could have died without a murmur; yet at the thought of being flogged like a dumb beast his whole soul revolted.

In a short time a shout from the rebels announced that the arrangements for tying him to the tree were all completed, and in a few moments he was borne in the arms of some half a dozen of them, and placed upon his feet at the foot of a small pine directly in front of the house. His coat and vest were then stripped off, and he was securely bound to the gummy trunk, with his back outward. A pile of slim green limbs of sufficient size to inflict a bitter wound was then placed by his side. A loud call from William then summoned his companions to witness the "sport," as he was pleased to term it. In a short time the whole squad was again around their prisoner, all wearing looks of infinite satisfaction. Up to this time Marvin Wilson had not spoken a word. He knew from the first that nothing short of an interposition of Providence could save him from his punishment, and he resolved to bear it in silence. But when he saw the arrangements for his torture all complete, and the process about to commence, he could not refrain from saying a few words. Turning his head from the tree as well as his bonds would permit, he caught the surly eye of O'Kane, and to him he addressed himself.

"O'Kane," said he, "this quarrel seems to have been between you and me. I own I am completely in your power, and I am willing you should enjoy the advantage; but for God's sake, if you are determined to wreak your vengeance upon me, do it like a Christian, and not in this brutal and barbarous manner. Shoot me, if you please, or hang me."

"Hear the whining cur!" replied O'Kane, addressing himself to his friends, not even deigning to notice his prisoner. "What's become of the fellow's courage, of which he made such pompous boasts but a few minutes since? Now he's as chicken-hearted as a woman."

"That's the truth," cried Hughes, stepping up to the pile of whips and selecting the largest he could find. "I'll teach him a lesson, though. I claim the first privilege at the dastard, as I received the wounds in securing him."

Hughes raised his arm, and was about to strike, when William shouted, —

"Hold, Hughes! let's call the girls, that they may witness the sport. The fellow has an enviable reputation as a gallant."

Hughes lowered his arm, and William hallooed loudly for the ladies. They rushed to the door, with the exception of Cora; but when they saw Wilson, and the brutal preparations with which he was surrounded, all, save Miss Rebecca, quickly retired. Hughes again approached the prisoner, and all was silent. He stood for a moment coolly selecting a spot upon his victim's back where he might most cruelly plant his first blow, and then he raised his sinewy arm and the blow descended. At the first stroke the blood bedyed the prisoner's shirt; but blow after blow, each succeeding the other rapidly, and each increasing in brutal force, fell upon his back, until Hughes was exhausted, and stepped back into the circle. Wilson's back was lacerated, and the blood flowed in streams; yet he uttered not a word. A few big and scalding tears chased each other down his cheeks, but not a muscle in his countenance moved. In a few moments after Hughes's blows had ceased, O'Kane stepped into the circle, and selecting a whip, thus addressed Wilson, at the same time preparing to participate in his torture: —

"What say you now, young brave? If I release you, will you huzza for Jeff Davis?"

"Never, by the eternal God!" replied Wilson, in a voice so calm, yet so concentrated, that O'Kane started as if he had been stung by an adder; and then, as if ashamed of the fear he had betrayed, he raised his arm and dealt Wilson a severe blow.

"What do you say now?" he asked again, grinding his teeth.

"As you give, you shall receive," replied Wilson, in the same calm tone as before.

"Bless me, but the fellow is game, after all," cried Hughes. "He threatens us yet. Huzza for Jeff Davis, my lad," he continued; "your back will thank you."

Wilson made no reply to this unfeeling speech, and O'Kane was about to continue his torture, when the sharp, quick cry of a dog caused all to start and to turn in the direction of the sound. The next moment the two dogs which had passed a short time before in pursuit of the deer dashed into the circle and began leaping and fawning upon their master. Wilson regarded them in silence, but the big tears coursed down his cheeks in rapid succession.

"Hang the dogs," cried Hughes; "don't let them stop the sport. Drive them from the ring."

No one stepped forward to put this threat into execution, and O'Kane struck the prisoner another blow. Scarcely had it descended, however, ere the dog that stood nearest his master seized the human brute by the throat, and hurled him to the ground. All instantly rushed to the rescue of O'Kane; and in the *mêlée* which ensued, a stranger emerged from the neighboring forest unobserved, and approached the scene of strife. He exchanged glances of recognition with Wilson, and then stood calmly surveying the scene.

The person of this stranger needs a particular description. His name is Archie Carter. By birth a Tennesseean, his father had moved to Texas when he was quite young. Here he remained until a few years previous to the opening of our story; and, as he loved the wandering life of a trapper, he pursued his game from forest to forest, and river to river, until we now find him on the banks of the Osage, a tributary of the Missouri. He was something of a military man, and had served under Walker, in the Mexican war, and had shown himself more than ordinarily brave at the battle of Palo Alto. In stature he was nearly seven feet, and of noble, nay, gigantic proportions. His face was the personification of homeliness; yet any one acquainted with physiognomy could easily discover in its coarse lines the marks of keen sagacity, dry humor, and genuine feeling; and these marks did not belie his character. His eye was a piercing gray one, surmounted by heavy eyebrows, which looked as if they had been planted helter-skelter by Dame Nature, and never had experienced the benefits of cultivation. His hair was coarse, and slightly gray, cut short, and, from its appearance, each hair seemed to be possessed of reason, and to stand in utter fear and abhorrence of its neighbor in either direction. In short, as the individual himself expressed it, "each hair was on its own hook." His nose, which was large and prominent, bore visible marks of hard service, as it possessed two distinct crooks, of such peculiar conformation as denoted that they were *knocked* into existence. His mouth was capacious; and when his lips parted, they disclosed two rows of teeth that would, to all appearance, laugh at shark's-meat steak or sea-biscuit.

His dress was as singular as his figure. It consisted of a cap of dressed deerskin, around the top of which were suspended several fox-tails, and a short jacket, or roundabout, as they sometimes were called, the lower extremities of which did not reach his waist into nearly a foot. The sleeves were also nearly six inches too short, leaving a full display for a wrist and fist which Archie was pleased to denominate as "Death's pestles." Like Joseph's coat, his was also, either from choice or necessity, composed of many colors. His pantaloons, which fitted his person closely, were made of buckskin, and, like their fellow-garment, were "too short altogether." Unlike most of the trappers, he did not wear moccasins; but his feet were protected by boots of the hugest and heaviest dimensions. On his arm lay a rifle of remarkable length and weight, and a powder-horn and pouch, together with a tomahawk and knife, found lodgment around his waist.

So intent were the rebels on loosing the grasp of the dog from the neck of O'Kane, that they did not observe the approach of Archie. After exchanging glances with Wilson, as before stated, he brought his rifle to the ground, and stood leaning his chin upon the muzzle, and quietly viewing the scene. The dog's grasp was at length broken, and O'Kane, who was not materially injured, arose from the ground, foaming with rage. The first object that his eye met was the figure of the above-described. He stood for a few moments like one thunderstruck, intently gazing at Archie. The eyes of the whole assembly followed his, and all were equally amazed. At length O'Kane found utterance, and he exclaimed, —

" Who the devil are you ? "

Archie gazed at him coolly for a few moments, and then replied, in a remarkably heavy voice, —

" What business is that of your'n, eh ? "

O'Kane was for a few moments speechless again; but at length he replied, —

" Don't be uncivil, sirrah, or I will have you arrested. These are suspicious times."

" Wal," replied Archie, "then don't you be sarsy, or, d—n me, I'll box your ears for you."

O'Kane saw that the imperturbable stranger was the wrong man to intimidate, and he changed his policy.

" My friend," said he, soothingly, "you know that suspicion is a natural attendant upon such times as these, and you cannot blame us for inquiring into your business here at this particular time. You may be friendly to us — "

"Don't call me your friend, you infernal scoundrel, or I'll cut you up in no time!" interrupted the stranger. Then suddenly starting, as if from a reverie, he approached Wilson, exclaiming, as he did so, —

"Marvin, my lad, this looks very suspicious. Why, your back looks like a ragged steak! I'm inclined to opinionate that somebody'll make up for this biz'ness, or I'll eat an airthquake!"

While delivering himself of this apparent parenthesis, Archie had unsheathed his knife and cut the cords that secured Wilson. Faint from suffering and loss of blood, the young man sunk at the foot of the tree the moment he was liberated; and Archie immediately dropped upon his knees by his side, and supported his head.

"Marvin, my boy," said he, "cheer up; don't be discouraged at this. It'll be the worst misforting that ever happened to O'Kane, after all. You'll get over it presently. It aren't worth mindin'." Raising his head, and gazing at O'Kane with an eye of fire, he continued, "This is infarnal pretty biz'ness for human bein's, now, ain't it, you infarnal pale-gizzard imp of the devil? It's a manly thing, now, ain't it? Darn me, I'll — "

He suddenly stopped speaking, and, opening his capacious mouth to its utmost extension, he uttered a horrid yell, that caused the whole rebel body to start and turn pale. In a moment, a heavy trampling was heard in the woods, and, shortly after, some thirty-five armed men were in O'Kane's yard.

"Seize every one of the vile heathen!" shouted Archie; "and one of you run for some water. We'll see how they like the reverse of their noble warfare."

In a moment, O'Kane and his guests were seized, and some dozen of the new comers were searching the premises for ropes with which to secure them. These were quickly found; and the rebels were soon lying upon the grass, as securely bound as Wilson had been a short time before. They made no resistance; for they saw it would be in vain. Indeed, from the very moment they discovered Archie, they appeared to be spell-bound — none having offered to interfere while he was releasing Wilson, even O'Kane himself remaining a passive spectator of the scene.

Archie soon succeeded in restoring Wilson to consciousness, and immediately set about dressing his wounds, at which business he appeared an adept. He appeared also to have every necessary material for this business close at hand, and in a short time he had performed the operation to his satisfaction. Calling one of his command to his side, he said, —

"Go into the house and get a shirt for the boy, and be quick about it. Get the best one O'Kane has got."

The man soon returned, and Archie completed his attentions to the patient. Leaving him at the foot of the tree, he proceeded to make other arrangements for the final disposition of his prisoners.

CHAPTER IV.

IN obedience to the orders of Archie, O'Kane and his companions were soon tied to the shade-trees of the yard, where they were left by the Unionists to ponder upon the sudden change in their fortunes, whilst they sought in the house for something to satisfy their hunger, guided, in the mean time, by their tall leader. As might be expected, the advent of the hungry crew into the sanctum of Miss Rebecca raised all the ireful feelings which she possessed. Through all the punishment of Wilson, and up to the sudden change in the situation of her friends, Miss Rebecca had maintained her post at the door, a witness of the whole. When, however, Archie spoke to his comrades about eating at the expense of O'Kane, she hastily retreated to her kitchen, and, arming herself with a tea-pot, in order to show as much contempt as possible for the Unionists, and to show them her independence of mind, she awaited their approach as calmly as a thunder storm awaits its appointed time. She was not compelled to wait long. In a few moments they came pouring in, headed by their tall leader, who was compelled materially to lower his crest, in order to enter the doorway.

"O, you marauding elves! O, you villains that you are!" cried Rebecca, directing her glaring eye towards the leader. "Eat at O'Kane's expense, eh! — will you?"

"Haw! haw! haw!" roared the tall captain, throwing himself into a chair. "Get us something to eat, you vinegar-faced beldam. Don't you s'pose we're as hungry as your friends was?"

"Vinegar face, eh! vinegar face! you brute, you!" cried Rebecca, trembling with rage. "Take *that*, you impertinent devil!"

7

At the same time, suiting the action to the word, she hurled her china tea-pot fair at the head of Archie, which conspicuous mark it missed, and was dashed into a thousand fragments against the wall.

"Haw! haw! haw! you old porcupine!" continued Archie; "you're a ra'al bruiser!" 'Pon my word, I should like to argufy with you; but I hain't got time."

Then, turning himself towards a few of the black servants, who were standing near, he exclaimed, "Bring forth some food instantly, if you don't want to be eat up yourselves. No delay, now!"

The servants hastily prepared to obey his order; and Miss Rebecca, whose rage had been somewhat calmed upon witnessing the demolition of her china tea-pot, again commenced: —

"O! if I was only a man, I'd warm your jacket for you, you great —"

She was interrupted by another burst of Archie's hearty merriment; and, without giving her time to conclude her sentence, that worthy replied, —

"If you was a man! Haw! haw! haw! That's funny. I swow, you'd look worse than I do. 'Pon my word, I'm glad I've come across you; for your infernal old face has put me in a better humor with my own. Haw! haw!"

The tables from the yard had been brought in, and the servants had arranged upon it the cold remnants of the rebel feast, and such other eatables as offered themselves, which, being observed by Archie, he cried, —

"Come, boys, the sun's getting low. Let's refresh, and do our business; for we've some ways to travel yet to-night. Corp' Smith," he cried, turning to an individual who stood near him, "take some of the best you can find to Marvin. It may do him good."

The man proceeded to execute his commission, and the remainder gathered around the tables. Rebecca stood watching their operations for some time in sullen silence; but at length she exclaimed, —

"I wish I had some *ratsbane;* 'pon my word, I'd pizen all of you — every one of you — and *you* in particular," said she, directing her eye to the tall leader.

"Haw! haw! you old fool!" shouted he, "do you think you could pizen me with ratsbane? Why, I've eat a peck on't afore now, to sweeten my stomach with!"

4

A general roar from the company followed this announcement, and Rebecca, seating herself in silent despair of gaining the contest, threw herself into a stiff attitude and remained silent, whilst Archie and his men concluded their meal. As soon as their repast was over, they all adjourned to the yard, to make a final disposition of the prisoners. After gazing at them for a few moments, Archie, signifying to his men that he wished for silence, thus delivered himself to O'Kane, before whom he was standing : —

"O'Kane, I'm a Christian individewl, and I, in gin'ral, deal with all my enemies in a Christian manner. My name is Archie Carter ; and I'm a Union man, as the Lord very well knows. If I had anything like a commission from Old Abe, I'd shoot every devil of ye in a Christian-like manner ; but you see I hain't got none yet, and I won't murder no way. You've disgraced human nature this day a little the hardest ! You've flogged a young fellow in a cruel and onnatural way, 'cause he differed with you in opinion. Remember, if I should ever meet you again with your cursed rebels, — remember my Long Tom," at the same time extending his rifle towards O'Kane.

Archie now prepared to march. A litter was constructed of some materials nearest at hand, for the purpose of transporting Marvin Wilson ; but, as he was about being placed upon it, Archie espied a skiff at the extremity of the yard.

"Hold on !" he shouted. "Place Marvin in the skiff, and I'll row it myself, while the rest of you take the shore path."

The new arrangement was acceded to, and in a few moments Marvin Wilson was conveniently placed in the skiff, with his faithful dogs beside him, and Archie prepared to manage the boat. The company started on their way, going by the shore path, under the command of Corporal Smith, while Archie shoved off the skiff, leaving the rebels still bound to the trees. As the skiff was shoving off, Marvin faintly turned his head towards the windows of the house, in order to catch a glimpse of Cora ; but she was nowhere to be seen. With a sigh he reclined himself in the boat, and was in a few moments beyond the scene of his late disaster.

When the strife between loyalty and treason was in its incipient stage, Archie was found upon the Union side of the question, and entered into the spirit of the Union movements with his whole soul. As has been intimated to the reader, he was now on a march with a company who had volunteered their services to "secure a license to fight," as he termed a commission, and then to go wherever his services were most needed. Those under his temporary command were nearly all young men from the vicinity of Osceola, and were destined for headquarters, to offer their services to the cause of Freedom. Accident had brought him to the neighborhood of O'Kane's, and the result is known to the reader. He had long known Marvin Wilson, as, indeed, did all the Unionists in that region of country; but Archie, in particular, for reasons which will be developed to the reader as he proceeds in the narrative, regarded him with warm and earnest affection.

As they proceeded down the river towards the young hunter's residence, he detailed to Archie all the particulars of his encounter with the rebels at O'Kane's. He had started early that morning in pursuit of game, not caring which way his course should shape, until at last his dogs aroused a noble buck, which started in the direction of O'Kane's. For some distance he followed his dogs with all the speed he could command; but as they were soon lost to his sight, he followed more leisurely, until he reached the house. The reader is already acquainted with the incidents that occurred there.

The sun was just setting when the skiff arrived at the cabin of Wilson, and in a short time afterwards the men who had followed the shore also arrived. After a brief consultation, they resolved to rest for the night where they were, and be governed by circumstances as to their future march. The cabin of Wilson could accommodate a part of them, and the balance could easily find lodging-places in the surrounding forest, as the weather was warm, and their limbs unused to the luxuries of feather beds and other like conveniences. After helping themselves to refreshments from their well-stored haversacks, they proceeded to search for convenient resting-places; and, soon after nightfall, all, save Archie, who was in Wilson's cabin, and one or two who were holding watch outside, were in the arms of Morpheus.

Miss Rebecca watched the disappearance of Archie and his men; and after waiting for some time, lest they should return, she then proceeded to call the female portion of her guests, who, from the first moment of Wilson's punishment, had sought refuge in a chamber, where they had remained during the whole affray, to come to

her assistance in the task of freeing her friends. They timidly
obeyed the summons, and, marshalled by the valorous dame, and
armed with knives, proceeded to liberate the sullen-looking band
who were tied to the trees in the yard. After they had all been
released, O'Kane, in the height of anger, swore eternal vengeance
on all Unionists, and especially upon Archie and Marvin Wilson.
He then turned to Sergeant Hughes and his men, and proposed, as
they had a long distance to go, that they should stay until morning,
which suggestion they concluded to acquiesce in.

The next morning, O'Kane began to make preparations for leaving home, for the purpose of seeing what could be done about re-
cruiting his guard. At sunrise, the sergeant and his men started
for the headquarters of General Price; and as they rowed their
boat into the middle of the river, they concluded it was not expedi-
ent to have the bonnie blue flag floating from its bow, thinking
that, under the circumstances, discretion was the better part of
valor. After O'Kane had made the necessary preparations for his
departure, he cautioned his servants to keep a good lookout, while
William supplied them with a few rusty old muskets and a little
ammunition; and Sambo, Jim, and Thomas thought themselves men
of some consequence. Their horses were now brought to the door,
and O'Kane and William mounted, and rode at full speed to the
residence of McBride.

The sun was going down as they entered the avenue leading to
the house of McBride. As they rode up to the door, McBride
met them; and when they had dismounted, he ordered a servant to
take charge of their horses, and bade O'Kane and his son to walk in.
He now caused a substantial supper to be prepared for them, to
which they did ample justice. Supper being finished, they were
invited into his library. After they were seated, he related to them
the news of Frost's surrender, and that he had received an order
from Governor Jackson to gather as fast as possible the friends of
the Confederate cause in this section of the state, and that he had
despatched circulars to the Knights of the Golden Circle, notifying
them that their presence was required at Clinton.

"The day appointed for the meeting is to-morrow," said he;
"and I am very glad that you are here, colonel; for you can accompany me to Clinton. We intend to have the Circle meet early
in the morning, and at ten o'clock in the forenoon we shall have a

public meeting, the object of which is to induce the non-slaveholding whites to array themselves upon our side; and you, O'Kane, must be one of the speakers. You must dwell emphatically on that point which will naturally touch their hearts; and that is, that the old despot in the White House is now preparing to march his minions into our state to destroy, ravish, and plunder the poor people, and that upon their banners is inscribed, ' Beauty and Booty.' "

Now that the programme had been made out for the following day, O'Kane and William interested McBride by relating to him their adventure with Wilson and Archie, and conversed until a late hour, when they all retired for the night. McBride, O'Kane, and William were on the road to Clinton as early as four o'clock, and arrived in time to transact all necessary business with the Circle. At ten o'clock the people assembled, and it was as motley-looking an assemblage of men as ever congregated together. O'Kane's eloquence had the desired effect, and after the meeting books were opened for enlistments. We here leave O'Kane and his son for the present, busily engaged obtaining names for his special guard.

When Cora O'Kane was led into the house after fainting in the yard, she immediately sought the quiet of her own chamber, refusing the company of several who offered their services to her. Her room was in the front part of the house, with one of the circular windows overlooking the yard. Once or twice, as she heard the shouts of her uncle's guests, she attempted to go to the window, and see what could be discovered; but her courage failed her. She did, however, finally glance at the yard. What to make of the appearance of the armed men that she there saw, she was utterly at a loss. She caught a view of Marvin Wilson, seated at the foot of the tree; and, not knowing what had previously taken place, she came to the conclusion that the assertion of O'Kane in relation to the plot in which Marvin was engaged was in reality true; yet her prejudices in favor of Wilson soon banished such thoughts. She retired from the window, and threw herself upon the bed. Here she remained until the noise occasioned by the departure of the guests again attracted her attention, and her curiosity got the better of her determination. She again went to the window, and found that her uncle's guests were departing. She concluded that nothing serious had occurred; and, feeling much easier under this conclusion, she again sought her couch.

She was not permitted to remain long in quiet, for she soon heard the voice of Miss Rebecca upon the staircase, requiring her presence below.   She obeyed the summons, and found her aunt in a terrible rage at the singular and unexpected termination of the day's business in general, but more particularly did she mourn and fume over the loss of her tea-pot.   If Cora was in ignorance of most of the transactions of the afternoon when she left her chamber, she did not long remain uninformed; for the exceedingly supple tongue of her aunt glided over the whole narrative with the speed of a locomotive, adding, besides a detail of the facts, several slight and pointed embellishments, for which the good dame was somewhat famous. Cora came in for a full share of the virago's vituperation, in connection with the Union partisans; and then, as if to inflict still more deeply her vengeance, Rebecca dwelt with peculiar earnestness and warmth of expression upon her detail of the punishment inflicted upon Wilson.   She described the appearance of his mangled back with great gusto, and wound up that part of her history by expressing a hearty wish that every Union man might meet with similar treatment at the hands of the Confederates.

The narrative of Rebecca filled the mind of Cora with dread and foreboding.   She saw that a rupture had indeed commenced, and what its fruits were likely to be was forcibly brought home to her understanding.   She loved Marvin Wilson.   She had not acquainted him with the fact by a *bona fide* assertion, but she had for some time admitted the fact in her communings with her own feelings. They had met but a few times, and then it was under circumstances extremely unfavorable to a development of the affections, or for an interchange of sentiment.   But it needs not opportunity or advantages to hear and understand the language of the affections.   A look or a tone, a smile, or some little, almost unnoticeable, movement is eloquent, and reveals more than the most learned and elaborate specimens of logic or eloquence could effect.   After Miss Rebecca had unburdened herself of her spleen, Cora was left again to herself.   She soon retired to her couch, to ponder upon what she had learned, and eventually to dream of him in whose welfare she now felt a deep concern.

CHAPTER V.

●

In the early morning Archie and his men were astir, and, breaking their fasts, they proceeded to hold a consultation as to what their future operations should be. Marvin Wilson had passed a sleepless night, and was suffering more from the wounds upon his back than he had the previous day. It became apparent to Archie Carter, despite his encouraging addresses to his patient, that his case was a critical one, and that he needed close attention and care. He could not, therefore, think of quitting the couch of his young friend; and he consequently proposed that the men, with the exception of two besides himself, should go to Clay's Settlement, and await the final issue of Marvin's illness, before proceeding farther on their intended journey.

" You know, boys," said he, in support of his plan, " it will never do to leave Marvin in this situation; for, setting the meanness of the thing to one side, we can't very well spare him just at this time."

The men readily assented to this plan, and all, save two specified by Carter, started, under the command of Corporal Smith, for Clay's Settlement, there to rendezvous until further deliberation. Clay's Settlement was but a few miles below Wilson's cabin, and was situated upon Grand Creek, which is a tributary of the Osage. It was quite a village, numbering several hundred souls, most of whom were warm and ardent Union men. They were convinced of the final event of the quarrel between the friends of the Union and those who were attempting to destroy it, and feeling a determination to be found ready when the storm should come, the men built for themselves a fort. They were sure of finding friends and a rendezvous at this place; nor were they disappointed in their expectation. When they informed the inhabitants that they were volunteers for the army of freedom, they were received with open arms, and were soon comfortably quartered in the Settlement.

Archie Carter was unwearied in his attentions to Wilson. He watched over him with an unusual tenderness, anticipated all his wants, and was incessant in his application of the medical herbs with which the forest abounded, and which his experience had taught him were salutary. Under his treatment, in a few days Wilson began to mend. They were supplied with provisions from the river and forest by the two men who remained with Archie, and, considering all the circumstances, Wilson's situation was not extremely unpleasant. In about three weeks' time he had so far recovered as to be able to undertake a day's hunting in company with Archie, being tired and weary of his long confinement.

It was a bright and balmy morning upon which they set out upon their excursion, and unthinkingly they shaped their course up the river, in the direction of O'Kane's. They followed the banks of the stream, and were already some four miles from their cabin ere they thought of a halt. Marvin, now growing faint, sat down at the foot of a tree, while Archie gazed attentively into the woods. At that moment he discovered a female coming towards them. She did not notice them until she was almost upon them. She then stood transfixed: she could not move a muscle, she was so frightened; but when she discovered that one was Marvin, she became more reconciled. Marvin, not dreaming that he should meet Cora, and now that he had so unexpectedly, felt his whole frame thrill with ecstasy.

As the reader is already aware, he loved Cora. His opportunities to converse with, or even see, her, were " few and far between." He had often resolved to tell her of his passion; yet up to the present time he had not spoken to her upon the subject nearest to his heart. The glance, however, which she gave him in the yard had caused him to form such a determination anew, should an opportunity favorable for the task ever occur. Now that the time had come, he resolved to unburden his mind. Archie knew full well how dearly Marvin would prize a private interview with Cora; and he, unperceived by Cora, wandered into the forest, out of view. Now that they were alone, Marvin addressed her. They sat for an hour or more, engaged in a desultory conversation, before Marvin ventured to make his declaration. At length he said, —

" Cora, I make no disguise or preliminaries. I love you — have loved you since I first saw you; and, knowing all the unfavorable circumstances by which I have been surrounded, here venture to throw myself upon your generosity. Tell me, Cora, do I love hopelessly ? "

Cora spoke not for a few moments; yet it was evident to Marvin, who regarded her intently, that she labored under deep emotion. At length, however, she replied, —

"Mr. Wilson, I will not deny that you are — that I do regard you with more than a common interest; and I will not deny, that, were circumstances different with me from what they now are, I could — "

Her tears impeded her utterance, and in a moment Marvin was by her side.

"Pardon me, Cora!" he exclaimed; "I have unthinkingly wounded your feelings. I should not have spoken to you upon this subject at this time."

"It is not that, Mr. Wilson," responded Cora. "If you only knew the wretchedness of my situation at home, you would at once comprehend all."

Cora then proceeded to detail to Marvin the treatment she received from her uncle and cousin, not concealing anything save the taunts inflicted upon her for the sake of him. Marvin's eye kindled at the tale, and he at once proposed that she should never more enter her uncle's door.

"I have but a poor house to offer you," he exclaimed, warmly; "but we can go where there is a better. I am not exactly what I seem; that is, I am not compelled to follow the avocation of a hunter for a livelihood. But consent to become mine now, and you shall be effectually rid of your uncle's persecution."

"That would never do," replied Cora. "I am entirely in his power until I am eighteen, and then, according to my father's will, I am free to do as I choose."

"It's a long time yet ere that privilege arrives," said Marvin, in a mournful tone, — "a long time, and, to my mind, freighted with important and mighty events."

"It is not so long a time," replied Cora. "For the sake of the prospects beyond, I can suffer till it rolls around."

They conversed for some time, and at last Cora proposed returning home. She was in the act of shaking hands and bidding Marvin good by, when she looked up and beheld William coming towards them on horseback. He rode by them in silence, and Cora proceeded slowly towards the house. Archie, all this time, was lurking around in the woods, when, hearing the sound of a horse's feet, and thinking something might be up, he rushed for the place where he left Marvin and Cora. Now that Cora had gone, Marvin and Archie returned to the cabin.

5

After arriving at the cabin of Wilson, Archie securely moored the skiff, and they retired within. It was here that Archie informed Wilson of his determination of visiting Clay's Settlement on the following day.

"There's no mistake," said he; "the devil's to pay among the rebels. That O'Kane affair must have made a noise. Here we've been caged up these three weeks and better, and hain't had a chance to gain a morsel of intelligence."

"That's true," replied Wilson. "It's high time we knew something of the movements of our enemies. So we'll even go to the Settlement."

The remainder of the day was spent by Wilson and his companions in arranging for their intended journey on the morrow, and in devising plans for their future operations. They retired early to their slumbers, intending to start for the Settlement with the dawn.

CHAPTER VI.

COLONEL O'KANE remained in Clinton four days, and during that time he had mustered into the Confederate service two hundred men, that were to be designated as the Missouri Confederate Guard. He had appointed his subordinate officers, and now they only wanted arms and ammunition to be ready for service. William had returned home two days before his father left Clinton, and was on his way there when he saw Cora and Marvin by the roadside; but he said nothing to her upon that subject when she had returned home a little while after. He had concluded to say nothing about it' until his father returned. When his father arrived, he told him what he had seen. O'Kane's anger knew no bounds. He said to William, —

"Cora must marry you immediately; and as for that d—d cur, Wilson, when my Guard arrives, under command of Lieutenant Colonel Rice, we will rid the country of his presence. My orders are to shoot every man who will not swear allegiance to the Confederate government. I expect my Guard to arrive here to-morrow; and you are appointed my adjutant."

O'Kane now left the room, and William was alone. He did not like the plan of going into the field, or into any active service with his father; for he was a consummate coward. Still, as all the young slaveholding aristocracy had enlisted, he could not very well but follow suit.

O'Kane, on leaving the presence of William, passed into his library, staid there but a few moments, and then went directly to Cora's room. She was sitting near the window when he entered, and immediately arose and tendered him a chair.

"I do not wish to sit," was the reply to her proffered civility.

He paced the little chamber several times uneasily and rapidly, and then, turning towards Cora, who, terrified at his singular behavior, had resumed her seat, he said, —

"Cora, for the last time I ask you, will you consent to marry William? This night you must choose, and your decision is to be final for this world. You had, therefore, better ponder upon it well. Again I ask, will you have William for your husband?"

"Uncle," replied Cora, trembling, — "*dear* uncle, I cannot wed him. Do not ask me."

"Have you decided?" asked her uncle, in a voice of forced calmness.

"I have, dear uncle," said Cora, embracing his knees and looking up into his face, while the tears rolled down her cheeks. "I can never marry him; but I *can* and *will* be his friend. Let that suffice."

"Away!" cried O'Kane, fiercely; "away! you need never attempt to practise your female arts upon me. No endearing appellations, no tears, can drive me from my purpose. Hear me again! You either marry William, or you die!"

Cora sank upon the floor speechless at this announcement. Her uncle regarded not her situation, but, hearing no reply, he continued, —

"Yes, you die! I swear I will not be balked by a silly girl. Come, rouse!" he continued, pushing her with his foot at the same time, "rouse up, and decide! Do you still say no?"

Cora had in some measure recovered from the shock which the violent conduct of her uncle had caused her, and she was therefore enabled to comprehend his last question. She feebly answered, "No," and O'Kane turned on his heel, and abruptly left the apartment, locking the door, and placing the key in his pocket. Cora remained lying upon the floor for nearly an hour, and then she arose and sought her bed. She deeply regretted that she had not taken the advice of Wilson, and left her uncle's roof forever. She felt sure that the latter would take desperate steps to force her to a compliance with his wishes. Then came the remembrance of his threat. She knew that she was not prepared to die. She thought of the secluded situation of her uncle's house — of how far she was removed from any one who would choose or dare to help her, and her heart sank within her. All the bright recollections of other days came thronging upon her memory, and she wept in bitter agony. All night long she was in tears; but when the day dawned, its blessed light cheered her, and she sank into a profound repose.

The sun was well up when she awoke, and, fearing the anger of her aunt, should she keep breakfast waiting, she arose hastily, and dressed herself with all expedition. She tried the door; but it was fastened, and the key gone. Finding all her endeavors to obtain egress vain, the poor girl seated herself by the window, to await, as she supposed, her final doom.

When O'Kane entered his library, he found there a courier from Governor Jackson. This courier was one of the most unrelenting rebels in Missouri. His name was Martin, and he had for many years been a slave-dealer. There was nothing so mean that he would not stoop to, to gain a penny. O'Kane, aware of this, after the message was delivered from Jackson, commenced the conversation by asking Martin if he was as discreet as he had been. Martin answered, that, so far as he knew, he was. O'Kane then said, —

"I have a little job for you, and will pay you well for it. It is this: I have a niece — the daughter of a deceased brother — residing with me, and it was the desire of that brother that my son should marry his daughter; but she declares that she'll die rather submit to it. Why she should have such an aversion to my son, I cannot conceive, only she is herself strongly in favor of the old Union, and is actually in love with one of the strongest Unionists in this vicinity. As I am going into actual service, and my house will not be guarded, those infernal Unionists might come and steal her away while I am gone. In order, therefore, to keep her within my power, I want you to take her this night and carry her to some safe and secure place within the Confederate lines, and I will pay you well for your trouble, and, of course, all necessary expenses while she remains in your custody. If she dies, so much the better; but do not murder her, nor do her any harm."

"It is not necessary," said Martin, "to carry her out of the state. I know a good many places where I can secrete her, where the devil himself can't find her; and I have one particular place in my mind now, where live an old uncle and aunt of 'mine. They are both the very strongest of Secessionists. They live in Pine-ville; but it is a mighty smart distance from here, .colonel. It is down near Arkansas; and the girl once there, I reckon she'll never trouble you again."

"Then," said O'Kane, "if you are willing to go to-night, I will make preparations for your departure at once."

"I had as lives go to-night as any time," said Martin. "The girl will have to carry her traps with her; for it is mighty hard getting things down there."

"I will see to all that," said O'Kane. "You will remain here until I return. I will not be gone long."

As he was leaving the room, O'Kane said, —

"I suppose you will take your own horse."

"Of course," said Martin.

Here O'Kane left Martin, and went directly to William, and informed him of his plan, and told him to go and arouse his trusty servant Sam, and have him harness Martin's horse into their light wagon. He ordered him not to lisp a word of what was going on. William was then to see his aunt Rebecca, informing her of his intentions, and requesting her to go to Cora's wardrobe, and select such clothing as she would need. He was also to help his aunt to prepare some food for the journey.

O'Kane then returned to the library, and informed Martin that his niece would be ready in a few moments. William now entered, and said that he had obeyed his commands, and that everything was ready. O'Kane immediately went up to Cora's room, rapped, and bade her rise, and open the door. Cora obeyed, and was in a short time fully dressed. Her uncle then commanded her to follow him down stairs, which she did, not, however, without fear and trembling. Arriving in the hall below, her uncle told her to go into the reception-room, and await his coming.

No one can describe the feelings of Cora as she was left there alone; but she was not left long to meditate, for soon in came O'Kane, Martin, and Rebecca, the last named of whom brought her travelling bonnet and other outside apparel, while her trunks were left in the hall. O'Kane addressed Cora, and said, —

"Inasmuch, miss, as you will not acquiesce in my wish in regard to marrying William, I am going to put you in charge of this friend of mine, who will carry you to one of his relatives. There you will be shut out from the world until such time as you are cured of your obstinacy, and will comply with my wish. And here let me warn you, as you love life, not to utter a sound as you leave these premises."

Turning to Rebecca, he said, —

"Assist the jade in dressing."

About one'clock Martin and his charge were on the road. Here we leave Cora pursuing her journey. It was nearly two o'clock before O'Kane retired to rest. He felt as though his mind was relieved of a great burden; and yet he felt sad, for a moment, as he thought of his conduct towards his niece. However, the thought of the immense fortune that he would receive, if Cora should die before she reached the age of eighteen, dazzled his eyes and crushed his better feelings, and he became more reconciled; for he felt sure Cora could not escape from the clutches of Martin, and that he could now have the assurance to write to Cora's bankers, and draw on them, if it should be necessary, under the pretence that she was dead.

The next morning O'Kane's Guard arrived, Lieutenant Colonel Rice commanding. The rest of the day was spent in drilling, and preparing to march for Warsaw in the morning. At sunrise the drum beat for roll-call, which was quite amusing to the servants; but Rebecca was terribly frightened. She thought the Unionists had come, led on by Archie. Her conscience smote her for her actions towards Cora. She had seen some awful sights in her dreams the night previous.

In a little while, the officers appeared for breakfast. Rations had been prepared for the men, and distributed among them, and they were soon on their way towards Warsaw. Nothing occurred on the road worthy of particular notice. When O'Kane and his men reached Warsaw, which they did by a circuitous route, coming into the town from the north, he called on some of the leading Secessionists who resided there, and, with their permission and assistance, went to work laying out a camp of instruction, as if he would remain there a few days. Thus he busied himself in drilling his men and dividing them into squads — some to forage, others to reconnoitre.

Here he enlisted fifty more men; and, the citizens providing them with horses, they were to be attached to his guard as mounted infantry.

CHAPTER VII.

WHEN Marvin and Archie arrived at the Settlement, they were informed that General Lyon was at Jefferson City. Marvin proposed to Archie and the men to go on and join General Lyon's command. This suggestion they heartily indorsed and agreed to. On the march they concluded to keep off from the main roads as much as possible, as they had but very little ammunition with them. When they arrived at Jefferson City, General Lyon received them cordially, and proposed at once to organize them into a company, as he could pass over enough other Missouri recruits to increase their number to one hundred. This was done, and Marvin was commissioned captain, and Archie first lieutenant.

For a few days, Marvin was busily engaged in drilling his men and equipping them. One afternoon an order came to him from headquarters, stating that his company would be third in rank, — which would be, of course, the color company, — and was assigned to the Twelfth Missouri Regiment, Colonel Cook commanding. As soon as the regiment was prepared for duty, they were ordered to march in the direction of Warsaw, and watch the movements of Jackson, keeping a good lookout.

The little regiment marched undisturbed to Versailles. Here the colonel concluded to halt, and go into camp, as the weather was exceedingly warm. He remained here two days, threw out his pickets, arranged his camp guard, and sat down to rest. At nine o'clock on the evening of the second day, the drum beat to quarters, and all was quiet save the tramp of the sentry to and fro on his beat, as he kept the patient vigil of the night. At two o'clock, on the next morning, the pickets were driven in by the advance of an army of rebels, as they said. The long roll was now beat, calling them to arms, and the regiment formed a line of battle in front of the camp, in as convenient a position as circumstances would admit.

The day before the following scenes were enacted, one of O'Kane's mounted infantry had discovered Colonel Cook's regiment in camp. He immediately wheeled, and reported to Colonel O'Kane, who was approaching, that he had discovered some Union troops encamped, and that they were not at a great distance from them. O'Kane now reported to his subordinate officers what he had heard, and, with their counsel, determined to give battle. He aroused his men, who were bivouacked for the night, with the order to march as quickly as possible. So rapid was the march of O'Kane's men, that his mounted infantry drove in Cook's pickets as early as two o'clock in the morning.

At sunrise, both commands formed in line of battle, and in a short time the fight commenced. It is impossible here to describe or explain the intentions of the commanders, for after the first volley it became a hand-to-hand conflict. The Unionists, overpowered by the rebels, were forced to retreat, and each man was obliged to take care of himself. Colonel Cook and Archie barely escaped with their lives, while, unfortunately, Captain Wilson was taken prisoner.

O'Kane was so delighted at the result of the conflict, that his exultation knew no bounds; but his joy was suddenly turned to sorrow when he learned that his son was among the slain. When the prisoners that had been taken were arrayed before O'Kane, to his great astonishment and delight he discovered among them Marvin Wilson. Preparations were now made by O'Kane to bury the dead and take care of the wounded. When this was done, they marched back to Warsaw with their prisoners.

CHAPTER VIII.

When O'Kane and his men had arrived at Warsaw, the prisoners were placed in a secure building, closely guarded, and his men went into camp, soon after which the assembly call was beat, calling the officers to the colonel's headquarters. After the officers had assembled, O'Kane thus addressed them : —

"Gentlemen, permit me to compliment you for your bravery in the fight. I have now called you for consultation in regard to the disposition of the prisoners we have taken."

It was agreed that they should be paroled, with the exception of Captain Wilson. O'Kane would not consent to have Marvin paroled, but did not give his reasons to his brother officers. He proposed that Wilson should be tried by court martial. The next day the prisoners were drawn up before headquarters and paroled. While this was going on, O'Kane ordered a squad of mounted men to go back and pick up all the straggling Unionists they could find. All this time Marvin remained alone in prison, closely guarded by a man whom he had known in the vicinity of Osceola, and from him he learned that Cora was either dead, or had been removed from this section of the country. The man said the general impression was that she was dead. All night long, Marvin's mind turned towards Cora, and often would he solioquize, —

"If she is dead, what is the use of my living? I am in the hands of O'Kane, and die I must; but I will die like a soldier. I should like to know what has become of Archie."

In this way he worried through the night. The next morning, the officers were again summoned to Colonel O'Kane's quarters, at which it was decided to postpone the trial of Captain Wilson four days.

After the order was given by Colonel Cook, on the day of the fight, that, as it was useless for them to hold out any longer, therefore every man must take care of himself, Archie, like an old veteran, at once made preparations to look out for Number One; and, so well acquainted was he with that part of the country, that he was not long in finding a hiding-place, where he felt perfectly secure from the observation of the rebels. He remained concealed until he felt sure that they had left the scene of action, and then slowly and cautiously did he move towards the field, to see if he could find the body of Captain Wilson, whom he supposed to be dead. The last he saw of him, he was in a precarious situation, fighting single-handed with four stalwart rebels; and he felt sure that Wilson must have fallen. Finding nothing of his body, he moved sorrowfully away. What to do next he did not know. As he stood meditating, one of his own men, who had also been concealed in the neighborhood, came to him, and told him that Captain Wilson had been taken prisoner; and this man also informed Archie that he had learned from the conversation of two rebels, who had passed his place of concealment on horseback, that the name of the rebel commander was O'Kane.

Archie at once came to the conclusion that it was all day with Marvin unless he could contrive some way to get him out of

O'Kane's clutches. " But how is this to be done? " said he to himself. " Here I am all alone, and not in a very comfortable place any how; but," said he, stretching himself up to his full height, " wherever there's a will, there's a way. The first thing I must do is to find a good gun. This little sword is good enough in its place; but I reckon it ain't just the thing for this undertaking. I let Corp' Smith have my old Long Tom. Blackberries and sugar! If I only had it now! I must stir about, and see what I can find."

After Archie had stood a few moments in meditation, he started off in quest of a gun. While roaming over the field, thinking he might perhaps find something that would answer his purpose, to his utter astonishment and delight he discovered among some debris on the field "old Long Tom." As he extricated the gun from the mass of rubbish partly concealing it from view, he exclaimed, —

" Wal, this is curious enough! Corp' Smith must be a goner. Now for a sufficient supply of ammunition, and I'm all right."

After Archie found himself perfectly equipped, he started in the direction of Warsaw. While plodding along, he discovered a negro cabin a short distance ahead. Stepping a little farther into the woods, and winding around, he cautiously approached the back side of the cabin, where he stopped and listened. Satisfied that no one was there, he ventured around to the front, and, seeing the door open, looked in. Observing no one but an old negress, he stepped in, and asked when she was last in Warsaw.

" O, massa! " replied the old woman, " a man is going to be tried and hung there, and my old man is coming home soon, and will tell you all about it."

" What has this man done, that they are going to hang him? " asked Archie.

The old woman, looking Archie straight in the face, replied, ' These are bad times, massa. Nobody knows their friends."

" That's so," answered Archie; " but I will be your friend if you will tell me."

" Wal, massa, all I knows of it is what Jim Thompson, a colored man that preaches to us, said. He told us that Massa Lincoln, away up north, was going to send an army down here to free us poor people; and that the army had come, and they have had a fight, and this man was taken prisoner, and they are going to hang him; and Jim said the curse of Almighty God would be upon them if they did so. Jim told us to go home and pray for him, and do all in our power for him."

" Wal," said Archie, " will you do it? "

" Golly, massa! I reckon I will."

" Wal," continued Archie, " I am that man's friend. I have come to help him, and shall try to rescue him from the hands of the rebels; and I want to find a place where I can remain in safety, to make preparations. Do you understand me? "

" O golly, massa! I think I can look through the whole of it. Come along with me, and I will show you a place where you will be safe."

. The old woman led Archie into the woods, and showed him the place where he was to take up his abode for a while. It was a cabin made by the uprooting of a large southern oak, and around it grew groups of little trees as thick as chaparral. A person would have to be well acquainted with the locality, to find the path leading to the cabin.

" You can remain here," said the old woman, " and I will bring you your meals. My old man will be home soon, and I will send him to you."

Archie felt happy, that, so far, he had succeeded so well. The old woman returned to her cabin, and found there the old man. She told him that a man had been there, and was now in the oak cabin. " Golly, Pompey! " continued she, " you think yourself big; but you are no size to dat man. He's come to help de man dat's in prison."

" Wal," said Pompey, " I'll go and see him right off. I see Jim Thompson to-day, and he said he'd been praying for the poor man all night."

The old man immediately went and saw Archie. When Pompey beheld his large figure, it made him stare. Archie informed him of his intention to rescue the man who was going to be hung, and said he wished Pompey's help.

" I can't help you much myself," said the latter; " but I'll go and see Jim Thompson right away, and have him come here this blessed night. He's the man that can help you."

Marvin remained for three days quietly and closely guarded. His room was large and well lighted, and the only privilege he had was to look out of the window, which was securely barred. The exercise which was allowed was in walking slowly up and down his room in constant meditation, and often would the joyous scenes of his boyhood pass in review before him. How melancholy did he feel when he saw all the inspiring anticipations of the future crushed forever, and himself cut down before he had reached the meridian of life! and yet more than once he detected himself planning some method of escape, or wondering if Archie was yet alive, and would not attempt his rescue.

In fact, he could not think of dying without a shudder; yet he had a clear conscience, and when he retired to rest his sleep was as sweet as childhood's. He knew that he was not confined for committing a brutal crime, but simply for defending his country, and devoting himself to the preservation of its institutions and liberties. As he was slowly pacing his room up and down, the officer of the guard entered, and said that the time of his trial would be on the morrow, at nine o'clock in the forenoon, and he must be prepared for it. Marvin bowed assent to the officer, who then left the room.

The next morning Marvin arose with the sun. It was a beautiful morning, although there was every indication of a sultry day. At a quarter before nine o'clock, the officer again entered the room, and informed Marvin that the time had arrived for him to march to headquarters for trial. Marvin then advanced towards the door, where he was commanded to step between the files of soldiers and march. The headquarters were situated at the hotel, some little distance from the house where he had been confined. As he marched along, the people pressed forward, eager to catch a glimpse of the prisoner; and among the crowd he observed one shining black face gazing upon him that gave him a thrill of hope.

When he reached the hotel, the people had surrounded the house, demanding admission; but this was objected to by Colonel O'Kane. Only a few of the more influential rebels were admitted. The main street was crowded with people, as never before had the town been so excited. The pent-up bitterness of the rebel heart was poured out in vehement curses upon the head of the prisoner. If there had been a man in the crowd around him that sympathized with him, it would have been madness and certain death to have given utterance to his feelings.

Some of O'Kane's soldiers were loitering about, and laughing over the success of their first fight, while others cursed Wilson, and exulted in his capture, and longed to see him die; and one that had a brother killed in the battle was heard to say that he wished the colonel would give him the privilege of disposing of him; he would tear out his heart, and the cracking of his bones would be music to his ears. When he had ended this speech, the coarse laugh of the soldiery might be heard at some distance, which told too well that they were all the slaves of sordid minds.

Marvin was marched into the room where sat O'Kane as the president of the court martial, with his clerk seated by his side. Marvin was ordered by the guard to be seated. For a few moments silence reigned. The clerk then ordered Marvin to rise, while he read the charges that were preferred against him.

"You, Marvin Wilson, are indicted on the following charges: First, when a member of the legislature, you refused to vote for the Military League Bill. Second, for opposing, and enticing others to oppose, the Confederate government. Third, for giving aid to the enemies of the state. Fourth, when war was upon us, you enlisted under the flag of our enemies, and were taken with arms in your hands."

"Guilty, or not guilty?" asked the clerk.

While the clerk was reading the charges preferred against him, Marvin stood gazing vacantly over the room; and, now that a direct question was put to him, he answered, —

"Guilty, if that be guilt."

The room was now cleared of spectators, and the prisoner taken back to confinement, while O'Kane and his officers remained to deliberate upon his fate. In about an hour Marvin was again sent for, and was once more removed to the hotel to receive his doom. It was filled with individuals anxious to hear the final determination of the inquisition. Marvin was marched in front of his judge, and the clerk proceeded to pronounce his sentence. It was death upon the scaffold. Two days were given to him to prepare for eternity. Marvin was asked if he had anything to say. He arose, and, turning to O'Kane, said, —

"Some in war are fortunate, others unfortunate; and I belong to the latter class. You may assume the authority to deprive me of life, but my soul will fly to the God who gave it. O'Kane, remember that there is a supremely just and righteous God, and, sooner or later, we shall both be summoned to appear before his judgment-seat. Then will you have to answer for this infamous deed that you are about to commit. This is all I have to say."

Marvin was removed to his old quarters, and the crowd within and around the tavern disappeared. O'Kane returned to his private room, but not, however, without feeling a sort of undefined symptom of uneasiness.

It was almost nine o'clock in the evening when Pompey made his promise good by bringing Jim Thompson to the white oak cabin where Archie was. The moon was shining so brightly that they could see each other while conversing. Archie inquired of Thompson if he was a friend to the man who was condemned to die. He replied, "I am, and this blessed day the soldiers took him out of Massa Robinson's house, where he has been shut up and guarded by soldiers, and brought him to old Mason's hotel to have his trial; and he is to be hung day after to-morrow, and I pray to God Almighty for help to set him free."

" Then," said Archie, " I want you to go with me this very night to Warsaw. I want to get as near Clay's Settlement as I can by daylight."

This Thompson agreed to do. In a little while after, Archie had cautiously passed the town. The next day, at nightfall, he reached the Settlement, and at once proceeded to arouse the settlers. Some thirty of them volunteered their services when Archie announced that the life of Captain Wilson was in danger, and that his person was in custody of the rebels. The settlers hastened to supply themselves with ammunition, and within an hour after the arrival of Archie they were prepared to march.

Archie and the settlers pushed on towards Warsaw with alacrity. The anxiety of Archie was so great for the fate of his friend, that he was constantly a few rods in advance of his comrades. They made such diligent use of their limbs, that just at night on the day after Wilson had been sentenced they came to a halt in a dark and almost impenetrable ravine, about half a mile below the summit of the little hill upon which the gallows was erected. The next morning after Marvin received his sentence he awoke from a refreshing sleep, infinitely better in health and spirits. Grief soon subsides, and the higher its flow, the sooner it ebbs. Marvin began to comprehend his situation; he thought over the scenes of the day before, and when he remembered that he was doomed to die on the morrow, his feelings experienced a shock that even the sentence of O'Kane had failed to give them. All this argued the return of a healthy state of mind as well as body.

When the guard again presented himself, Marvin preferred a request for writing materials, saying that he wished, in a measure, to arrange his business before he made his final exit from the stage of action; but this favor was refused, and he was left alone. In the afternoon, he was visited by the minister who officiated as chaplain of O'Kane's Guard, who came to administer to the prisoner the spiritual comforts of the gospel. The worthy individual talked for a long time upon the horror of treason to the state, and the unpardonable sin of rebellion against the government of the Lord's anointed. Matters assumed to Marvin a more serious aspect than they had seemed to wear. When the minister announced his errand, it appeared to bring death and himself into frightful proximity. There was something inexpressibly chilling to his feelings in coldly setting about making preparations for his final departure. He knew that preparation for so important an event was highly necessary, but, despite all his efforts, he could not bring his mind to think calmly upon the subject. The worthy divine left him, expressing his fears that his latter end would be worse than the first.

O'Kane rose early next morning, and began making preparations for the execution, which was appointed to take place early in the evening, just after the setting of the sun. How he came to designate this unusual hour as the time for the unhallowed sacrifice he intended to make he could not tell; yet he could not bring himself to perpetrate the diabolical deed with God's fair sun a witness to the transaction. He "loved darkness rather than light," and it was, undoubtedly, because his "deeds were evil."

The spot selected for the execution was just outside the compact portion of the village, on the side of a little hill which gently rose from the bank of a small streamlet. A rough, ill-constructed gallows was declared to be in a state of readiness a little past noon. An hour before the setting of the sun, one of the guard entered the room, and bade him prepare to march immediately to the place of execution. Marvin obeyed; and, when he emerged from the house, the armed rebels filed into a square, leaving him in the centre, and, led by O'Kane, bent their steps slowly to the little hill upon which the gallows was erected. A large concourse had collected here, to witness the approach of the condemned. A passage was cleared by the Guards on the arrival of the prisoner, and in a short time after he was seated on the gallows. The settlers were sent out upon the afternoon of the execution, and mingled with the crowd. When the cavalcade started for the gallows, they cautiously detached themselves from the multitude, and again sought their comrades. No time was to be lost, — a moment might thwart their intentions, — and Archie formed his men in order, and marched from the ravine towards the little hill. Just as Marvin mounted the scaffold, they came in view of the machine of death, and halted, in such a position as would, in all probability, owing to the intense interest in the execution, shelter them from observation. After his men were covered, Archie marched boldly up to the crowd, pushed his way through the Guard, and, mounting the steps, stood the next moment upon the scaffold, in front of O'Kane. Marvin uttered an exclamation of surprise; but, if an apparition from the world of spirits had stared him full in the face, O'Kane could not have been more completely thunderstruck. Many of the rebels well knew Archie Carter, — some of them to their cost, — and a suppressed whisper of his name soon ran round the crowd. The rebels looked fierce, and awaited orders from O'Kane; while a gleam of satisfaction was plainly to be seen upon the countenances of the Unionists, who crowded as near to the scaffold as they possibly could.

"What are you going to do, reprobate?" said Archie, bringing his heavy rifle down upon the scaffold with a force that caused O'Kane to start and turn pale. "What do you mean to do? Have you forgotten Archie Carter so soon?"

"I have not forgotten you, as you will find to your cost," said O'Kane, after he had in a measure recovered from the shock he had received from the unlooked-for presence of Archie. "At present we are going to adminster justice to a condemned criminal, and after that we will attend to your case."

"You administer justice!" cried Archie, furiously, shaking his huge fist in O'Kane's face. "You talk about justice, you skimmings of the devil's wickedness! Zounds! if I hain't a mind to string you upon this very frame, you miserable devil that you are."

A loud shout from the Unionists in the crowd attested their satisfaction at seeing the haughty O'Kane bearded in the presence of his minions. O'Kane was enraged beyond bounds, and shouted, —

" Seize the villain ! "

" So I will," interrupted Archie, at the same time depositing his rifle on the scaffold, and seizing O'Kane by the throat. " So I will seize the villain ; for may I be cussed if you ain't the man, if they's any such a one present." At the same time, Archie inflicted several severe blows upon his face ; then taking him with one hand by the leg, with the other remaining upon his throat, he threw him from the scaffold into the crowd below. Drawing his knife from his belt, he cut the cords which bound Marvin, and handing him the weapon, he said, —

" Defend yourself, my lad ; bless me, but we'll expalify the whole bilin' on 'em ! "

Seeing their leader assaulted in this unceremonious manner, several of the rebel Guard rushed towards the scaffold. But they were intercepted by a little knot of Unionists, who had taken post immediately in front of it. A warm scuffle here ensued ; but the Unionists, being few in number, were compelled to give way, and about a dozen rushed up the steps to secure Archie Carter. The frail platform could not sustain the accumulated weight of all, and with a loud crash it came to the ground. A moment afterwards, Archie uttered a loud yell, and the settlers came pouring down the hill from the ambush.

" Come on ! " shouted Archie, as he saw his men issue from the forest. " Come on, my lads, the victory is ours ! "

The women and children in the crowd ran screaming in all directions. The unarmed Unionists, uttering a shout, scattered also, to arm themselves as best they might ; and altogether the scene was one of confusion.

" Fire upon the pirates ! " shouted O'Kane, who had regained his feet, and was in a terrible rage. A part of his Guard instantly formed, and discharged a volley at the Unionists, two of whom fell to rise no more.

" Pepper 'em ! my boys ; pepper 'em ! " shouted Archie, in a towering passion.

The Unionists obeyed, and in an instant a sharp volley was discharged at their opponents, who, seeing several in their ranks sink to the earth, turned and fled in the direction of the village, pursued by Archie and his men a short distance.

In the morning, the bodies of those killed in the affray were

7

decently interred; and the men, accompanied by Captain Wilson and Archie, departed on their return to Clay's Settlement. When they arrived there, Captain Wilson received the congratulations of all on his providential escape.

CHAPTER IX.

As Martin drove swiftly away, Cora well knew that it would be useless for her to attempt a struggle, or raise an alarm, and she resigned herself to her melancholy situation, and bitter thoughts filled her mind. Martin urged his horse to the utmost speed. What was to be her fate she could not conjecture; she knew very well that her uncle meant her destruction by what he said in the hall. It seemed to her that she was sitting by the side of her murderer; for, when he was introduced to her, she came to the conclusion that he was a ruffian, hired to transport her to some convenient and isolated place, and there despatch her. At all events, she knew, even if that was the case, she was completely in his power; and she felt, in her inmost heart, that an appeal to his mercy would avail her nothing. Just as the day dawned they arrived at a small cabin a little way from the road. Here Martin halted in front of the door. He jumped out and tied his horse, then assisted Cora to alight, and ushered her into a narrow, dirty room. By his actions he appeared to be on familiar terms with the inmates of the cabin, and perfectly at ease. He instructed them to prepare breakfast, while he went out to give some provender to his horse; and here he discovered a basket of provisions, which he brought into the house. He then opened it, and put part of it upon the table, to help make out the meal. Breakfast being now ready, they sat down and partook of it in silence. After Martin had refreshed himself, he stepped out and gave his horse some water, and at the same time put his provisions into the wagon. He then stepped back to the door, and told Cora that he was ready. Helping her into the wagon, he drove leisurely along. For over two miles they rode without speaking. Then Martin broke silence, and said, " I am not going to murder you, nor insult your person; but, if you will keep your tongue to yourself, say not a word, it will be much better for you. To-night we will have to stop at a tavern, and I will provide a good room for you."

As they rode along, the heat of the sun became intense, and very oppressive to Cora. Martin, seeing this, stopped his horse, alighted from the wagon, and cut some green boughs that grew by the road-side, and placed them in such a manner as to shield Cora from the oppressive heat of the sun. The sun was nearly down when they reached the tavern. As Martin drove up to the door, a man came out, and said, —

"Well, Martin, how are you? What news up your way?"

"The war has come; and they are fighting right smart, I reckon," replied Martin.

By this time he had jumped out of the wagon, and handed out Cora.

"Pinkey, show this girl into the house, and have the old woman get us some supper, while I unhitch the horse."

The man ushered Cora into the house; and a poor apology for a tavern it was too. As soon as Cora had taken off her bonnet and outside garments, she inquired of the woman if she could have some water carried to her room, so that she might cleanse herself, as she was hot, tired, and dusty. The woman replied in the affirmative. Martin now entered, and said, —

"Pretty red day, Pinkey."

"I reckon," said Pinkey.

Supper being now ready, Cora and Martin sat down to their meal of pork, hoe-cake, and honey. After Cora had eaten, she went directly to her room. The room which she was to occupy was partitioned off from the main one, with rough cypress boards. As Cora closed the door, the woman said to Martin, —

"Right smart girl that."

"Yes," said Martin, "but born for heaps of bad luck, I reckon."

After Cora had overheard the remark of Martin, she concluded to keep awake, in the hope of hearing something in regard to her destination; but at length she felt a drowsiness creeping upon her. Despite her exertions to keep awake, she dropped her head upon her pillow, and fell asleep; and in the dreams of home she forgot the wretchedness of her situation. She slept until she was aroused by the woman in the morning. As soon as breakfast was de-spatched, Martin and Cora were upon the road. About noon they arrived at a small house, where they took dinner, and immediately resumed their journey. So adroit was Martin in the management

of affairs, that Cora found it utterly impossible to speak to any one
at the last stopping-place, and she proceeded on her way with a
heavy heart. Martin pursued the remainder of the journey with
the utmost speed, barely stopping for refreshments. On the evening of the third day after leaving Osceola, Cora was securely located
under the roof of Martin's relatives. On the day after her arrival,
she was visited in her room by Martin's aunt, a rough-looking woman,
bearing in her arms a coarse cotton home-made dress, which the
old woman commanded her to put on, in place of the one she then
wore. She was forced to comply, and the woman left her to pursue
her own amusement, if such could be found. All hope had entirely
deserted Cora. She could not even bring. herself to view her truly
deplorable situation with anything like patience or resignation. Shut
out entirely from the world, destitute of a companion, or even a
book, she was compelled to pass away the tedious hours in perfect
idleness; the most irksome situation that can well be imagined for
one so young, and naturally of so lively a disposition, as Cora.

All this time Cora's health was good; yet she sometimes prayed
for death, and often did she exclaim to herself, "I cannot endure
this torment much longer." Then she would think of Marvin, and
her heart would throb with the hope that she would be released, and
have the sweet pleasure of seeing him again.

One afternoon, as Cora was sitting in her lonely room, a stranger
entered the cabin, and commenced conversation with the old woman.
He conversed in such loud tones as to be overheard by Cora, who
crept to the door of her room to hear more distinctly. In his conversation with the old woman, he told her that the Union troops
were driving the Confederates right before them; "and it won't be
long before they will be here," he added.

"Sakes alive!" replied the old woman, "what shall we do then?"

"Wal," said the man, "we must get over into Arkansas, or remain and take the consequences."

Cora was glad to learn that the Union army was approaching,
and thought it might possibly be the means of her release; but,
finding the conversation had no allusion to her, returned to her seat.

After Marvin had been released from his perilous situation by
Archie and the band of settlers, the reader remembers that he accompanied Archie and the settlers to Clay's Settlement. Marvin
and Archie both concluded that it was their duty to join the Federal

army, which was then at Rolla, as soon as possible, which they did by marching through pathless forests. On the 26th of July, General Fremont arrived at St. Louis as Military Commander of Missouri and its adjacent territory. He found the army in depressed spirits. Many of the regiment's time of service had nearly expired. On the other hand, the rebels were in high glee, as they felt that Missouri would rise up and rally around the Confederate standard. The rebel commanders had ordered guerilla bands to be organized, to operate with vigor, night and day, until they had rid the state of every Union man ; and vigorously did they carry on their hellish work. General Fremont saw that something must be done to stop this cruel mode of warfare, and he organized companies for this especial service, consisting of one hundred men each. They were to be mounted infantry, and act independently of the rest of the army. Of one of these companies Marvin Wilson received the command, and Archie Carter was made second in command.

On the 1st day of August, this company marched from Rolla to Lebanon. At sundown they halted in front of a little cabin, where an old man came out, supposing them to be rebels, and told them that O'Kane, with four or five hundred rebels, was in the vicinity of Osceola. The company here bivouacked for the night. Next morning, Captain Wilson called his men by sunrise. They soon prepared a hasty breakfast, and were on the road towards Clay's Settlement. When Marvin and his men had reached the river, they discovered a skiff drawn up on the shore.

"Look here, Marvin," said Archie ; "here's O'Kane's skiff. I wonder if he's round these diggin's. I rather think we had better keep our eyes peeled."

Captain Wilson now ordered two men to ride down the river, to see if they could ascertain anything of the movements of O'Kane. They shortly returned and reported that all was quiet. Archie suggested to Marvin that Second Lieutenant Rollins should take charge of the men, and march them to Clay's Settlement, keeping back from the river as far as possible, while they should take the skiff and go by water. This Marvin assented to. In a few minutes, Lieutenant Rollins, with the company, marched. Marvin and Archie were soon on their way down the river. It was a glorious morning. The birds sang sweetly from the deep, rich foliage of the forest; the air was filled with the perfumes of a hundred different wild flowers; and stretching far away before them was a bright line of water, as smooth and unruffled as the sky above them. Archie labored at the oars, while Marvin sat at the stern of the little boat, drinking in the matchless beauty of the scene, and thinking of Cora O'Kane. Even Archie himself was sensibly touched by the splendid view about him. He rolled his eyes from side to side, gazing up at the tall trees on either hand with lips parted and nostrils extended; and more than once he ceased dipping his oars, as some new picture in the fairy prospect presented itself to his vision. He finally addressed Marvin in relation to the scenery around him.

"I tell *you*, Marvin, that this is a vast airth. Now, some folks pretend to say that woman is the greatest feat of God's workmanship; but, Marvin, it ain't so, no way. If there is any best to the Lord's craft, it's this airth that we live on. I've seen a good deal on't, Marvin, and I know it's *great!*"

"It is indeed a beautiful world," replied Marvin.

"Bootiful!" exclaimed Archie, with a strong expression of contempt upon his homely features. "Go way with your gal talk, man. I say it ain't bootiful: it's *vast*, it's mighty, it's big! It's made so a purpose, too. It shows that there's some one in existence that's got a mightier arm than Jeff Davis — some Spirit that even the haughty slave master must obey."

"That's true enough," said Marvin.

"True as Genesis," repeated Archie; "and I'll be cussed if I'd be a rebel just on that account."

"Why so?" inquired Marvin.

"'Cause it's blasphemy: no — a idolatry, I mean," said Archie. "I argy that no man can worship a human bein', as these men, called rebels, worship the slave-owners, without being idolatrous. Blast 'em, they ought to be sent to the missionary society, to get civilized!"

Archie continued to draw sage conclusions and arguments from almost everything that attracted his attention, and the consequence was, that the voyage proceeded but slowly. Once or twice Marvin ventured to hint that they should arrive late at their place of destination; but Archie paid no manner of attention to him, barely remarking, at one time, that he was determined to argue his point out, if the devil forbade him.

About ten o'clock they reached a place where the river assumed a lake-like form, shooting for some distance into the green forest on either side. Rowing to the shore on the southern side, Archie announced his intention of halting long enough to partake of his luncheon. As they had breakfasted early, Marvin was in no way disinclined to join him in this operation; and they both accordingly went ashore. As Archie was proceeding to unroll his rations from the cloth in which they were enveloped, a sound in the forest caught his ear, and he ceased from his occupation. He listened intently for some time, and then, rising upon his feet, he turned to Marvin, and said, —

"I guess we mought as well drag the skiff into the bay here, and throw a little brush over it, and then hide."

"Why so?" inquired Marvin, who had likewise assumed a standing posture.

"You'll see, I guess," said Archie, stooping to deposit his provisions upon the ground, and then going towards the skiff. "Come, let's be lively."

Marvin proceeded to assist him in hauling up the skiff; but, ere they had accomplished their task, a loud laugh in the forest caused them both to desist.

"We must let the skiff go, and look out for ourselves," said Archie, gazing around him in all directions for a place in which to secrete himself. Just across the arm of the river was a large pile of dried brush, which caught the eye of Archie, and he exclaimed, "Come, Marvin, it'll wet your breeches, but it can't be helped. We must go to that brush-heap."

Without further ado, Archie, holding his rifle in one hand and his provisions in the other, dashed into the stream, followed by Marvin. The water was but about three feet deep, and some eighty or one hundred feet broad; and they soon reached the opposite shore in safety, and then concealed themselves beneath the heap of brush. They soon heard the trampling of many men in the woods, and in a few minutes some thirty or forty whites, and nearly as many Indians, came into view a few rods to the east of where the skiff was lying. Here they all halted, seeming to entertain a similar opinion with Archie in regard to eating; for they immediately seated themselves upon the ground, and began to overhaul their stores, as if to supply the wants of nature. This band appeared to be under the command of a heavily-moulded man, who issued his orders to his men in a short, peremptory tone, and who sat apart, while partaking of food, in gloomy silence. The Indian warriors were headed by a heavy-featured half-breed, in whose eye the glance of a hundred devils seemed concentrated.

There appeared to be but little discipline among either whites or savages; for their merriment and conversation were loud and boisterous, and received no check from their taciturn leader. After their repast was concluded, some of the soldiers proceeded to stray about the forest, in the immediate vicinity of their halting-ground, while others stretched themselves on the ground, with their heads placed upon their knapsacks, seeming determined to rest while all things were propitious. Some six or eight of the strollers wandered in the direction of the arm or bay before mentioned; and one of them, espying the skiff, gave vent to an ejaculation which attracted the attention of his comrades to the same object. They were soon gathered in a group upon the shore, speculating upon the probable means by which the skiff came in that place, and giving utterance to various conjectures as to who its occupants had been, when one who had lagged behind his comrades came up, and, seeing the skiff, exclaimed, —

"I know that boat!   That's O'Kane's boat. I could swear to it in any place!"

"How the devil came O'Kane's boat here?" asked two or three at once.

"Probably they are hunting in the forest hereabouts," replied the individual who had spoken first.

"They have hauled up the skiff here, to remain until they are ready to return."

"What track is this?" cried another, stooping down and viewing the soft earth near the shore.

"It's the print of a stone-boat, you fool!" answered a comrade.

"What the devil would a stone-boat do here?" asked the stooping person.

"Eternity! what a foot!" exclaimed another; and in a few moments the whole group were viewing the print of Archie's trusty boot.

"The man that carries that foot can walk on the water," cried one of the men.

"How the devil can he get through the woods?" inquired another.

A loud laugh at this interrogatory issued from a dozen mouths; and then, as if satisfied with the observations that had been made, the knot separated and rejoined their comrades. They were soon again under arms; and, after a brief survey of the lines, the taciturn leader gave forth the order to march, and the whole band started off in the direction of Clay's Settlement.

Marvin and Archie continued in their hiding-place for a full half hour after they had departed, before they emerged. Archie was the first to crawl from beneath the brush; when, stretching himself to his full height, and yawning once or twice, he again seated himself upon the ground, and coolly proceeded to unroll his provisions. After he had displayed his food upon the ground in a manner that suited his fancy, he turned to Marvin, and said, —

"Some of them chaps was determined to be merry at the expense of my foot — warn't they, Marvin, eh?"

Without giving Marvin time to reply to this question, he continued, —

"He thort it was the print of a stone-boat; haw! haw! haw! Hang me, but he'd think 'twas the butt eend of death, if it should ever get foul of the hind part of his trousers."

"You have a little pride, I see, Archie, as well as the rest of the world," responded Marvin, laughing.

"Pride!" said Archie, his cheeks distorted with cold venison, at the same time glancing complacently at his foot, which was lying carelessly upon the ground. "Pride! I hain't got a bit; but then, captain, it's d—d onginerous to ridicule a man's parson, when he's jest as the Lord made him."

"True; but it's the fate of war," replied Marvin, half seriously.

Archie was just elevating a huge slice of brown bread to his mouth; but it ceased its upward motion and came to a halt as he replied, —

"The fate of *war*, Marvin! Why, bless me, man, I b'lieve you're love-sick. No, sir, it's no part of a warrior to ridicule a man's parson. I know I've got a big foot; but you must remember, sir, that I'm a team all over. I'm no small beer by a considerable of a great sight!"

Marvin admitted the truth of Archie's assertion, and they concluded their meal in silence. After it was finished, and Archie had gathered up and secured the fragments, they recrossed the bay, and

8

were once more afloat in the skiff, Archie merely saying that it was fortunate that they had found a hiding-place before the rebels perceived them. "'Case," said he, "we might have had a skrimmage!" Archie directed his skiff to the northern shore, and vigorously plied his oars.

They were not long in arriving at the confluence of the Grand Creek and the Osage, when they carefully secreted the boat, and pushed forward to the Settlement on foot.

Lieutenant Rollins and the men arrived at the Settlement about the same time with Marvin and Archie. They were joyously received by the inhabitants; yet they found them in the greatest state of alarm, and in momentary expectation of an attack from O'Kane's rebels, and a detachment of Pike's Indians who were temporarily under O'Kane.

The women and children were placed within the fort; the cattle were driven up into the yards; sentinels were posted in the forest around them in different directions, and everything that could contribute to a vigorous and determined defence was placed in some convenient situation. Captain Wilson and Lieutenant Carter detailed their meeting with the rebels and Indians in the woods; and the fact of their continuing their march in an easterly direction seemed to confirm their fears and suspicions of an attack.

Soon after sundown, all sought refuge in the fort, which, although not built in a scientific form, was sufficiently large and secure against the attack of any troop destitute of artillery.

In the evening, a consultation was called in the fort by the chief men in the Settlement, and Captain Wilson and Lieutenant Carter were of course called upon to participate in their deliberations. A plan of defence was agreed upon in case they should be attacked; and, as the inhabitants were well aware that they could not expect any mercy from the Indians, and scarcely any from the rebels, it was determined to fight until the last.

After the conclusion of the consultation, the guns and ammunition of all were closely inspected; and all but the sentinels on duty retired to rest.

All was silent and undisturbed until near midnight, when the sentinel stationed farthest in the forest to the west of the Settlement, discharged his gun, and hastily retreated towards the fort. The alarm soon spread, and in a short time every man in the fort was

under arms, and prepared for battle. They were not long in expectation; for, a few minutes after the sentinel who gave the alarm
had entered the fort, the troops seen by Marvin and Archie in the
morning, with a strong reënforcement that had joined them on the
way, made their appearance, accompanied by the Indians. As soon
as they were discovered, a burst of horror escaped the lips of several of the women in the fort, and the exclamations of " O'Kane! "
and " Pike's Indians! " were passed from ear to ear.

It was indeed those ruthless marauders, who continued, during a
portion of the rebellion, to heap more odium upon their heads than
ever before fell to the lot of individuals like themselves, who were
marching now to the attack of Clay's Settlement. They had been
strongly reënforced by a detachment sent on by General Price to
coöperate with them, and, panting for blood, and revenge upon the
Unionists, had approached the fort.

The name of O'Kane, and the presence of the savages, seemed
to strike a chill to the heart of every woman and child of the
Settlement.

At this moment, Captain Wilson and Archie formed their men in
such a position that they felt that it was impossible for O'Kane's
men to enter; so they let them approach within short range.
Lieutenant Carter now, in a voice of thunder, commanded his
squad to fire. Captain Wilson immediately followed the example
of Carter, and commanded his squad to fire. At this moment a
tall spire of flame, from a barn near the fort, cast a bright and
fearful glare over every object; and its appearance, and the tone in
which Carter spoke, served to arouse the settlers from their lethargy,
and they, in connection with the troops, who had reloaded, poured
in a close and deadly fire upon the advancing rebels.

The Indians now turned immediately, scattering in all directions,
and uttering wild and unearthly yells. A loud bellowing among
the cattle outside soon announced their whereabouts and occupation.

As no part of the soldiers' or settlers' persons was exposed, the
rebels did not discharge a gun; but, recovering from the slight
disorder into which the volleys of the Unionists had thrown them,
reformed, and steadily advanced towards the entrance to the fort,
headed by O'Kane. Ere they arrived there, however, another discharge — more deadly in its effects than the previous ones — caused

them to waver a moment; but, shouting, "Huzza for the bonnie blue flag!" O'Kane again advanced, followed by his men.

The burning barns increased in every direction. The cattle that had escaped the knives of the savages were running in the fields, and through the streets, bellowing furiously. The women and children within the fort were shrieking and fainting; and a more distressing scene than the assaulted Settlement presented at this time could not well be conceived.

The Unionists kept up a brisk discharge; but, as the rebels were close in under the walls, they were without any great effect. The doors of the fort were composed of heavy oaken plank, and against them O'Kane directed all his strength and ingenuity. A half dozen axes were incessantly playing upon them from without; while those within saw the utter futility of all attempts to block up the passage in case the door should give way, as it certainly must, under the vigorous efforts now going on to effect it.

Captain Wilson immediately selected a number of the most sturdy and determined of his command, and took his station directly in front of the door. He urged and exhorted his companions to a firm and unyielding resistance, and they promised implicitly to obey his orders.

In about half an hour the door fell in with a heavy crash, and the fierce combatants stood face to face — foe to foe. Uttering a cry of encouragement to his comrades, Marvin dashed upon the advancing column of rebels, dealing tremendous blows in every direction around him, with a huge sabre, which he had selected for that purpose. He was bravely seconded by his comrades; and, so impetuous was the onset, and so determinedly was it kept up, that, despite their greater numbers, the rebels were compelled to retreat. This change in circumstances was observed by Archie, and, shouting for the rest of the soldiers and the settlers to advance, he too rushed into the furious conflict. This accession increased their hopes, and consequently their exertions. They fought like heroes; and, notwithstanding O'Kane used every encouragement and threat that he could devise, his men continued to give ground.

A fierce and bloody conflict raged without the fort for nearly an hour, the rebels gradually retreating, and the Unionists following them up closely. O'Kane at length perceived the folly of continuing the battle; and he gave orders to his men to retreat to the forest, intending to rally again, and once more renew the encounter. They were pursued but a short distance by the Unionists, who, knowing that they would be conspicuous marks in the light of the blazing buildings around them, retreated to the fort, hastily collecting, as they did so, their wounded comrades. They immediately set to work to repair the fallen door of the fort, which they accomplished as well as they could in the hurry and confusion of the moment. A new supply of ammunition was dealt out to the men, and they awaited another assault from the discomfited rebels.

O'Kane was more than an hour in preparing and urging his men to another assault. The Indians had slaughtered all the cattle within their reach, and, thinking that such an honor was sufficient, refused to participate further in the conflict until the women and children were to be scalped.

O'Kane, however, was not to be intimidated or deterred from another attempt, and at length his men prepared, sullenly, to follow him again beneath the walls of the fort. Slowly and solemnly they marched in the direction of the fort, and approached even nearer than at first, before the Unionists evinced any symptoms that they knew of their whereabouts. Then, however, they were overtaken by a tremendous discharge, at which some dozen fell, while the remainder came to a dead halt. Another discharge quickly followed the first; when, breaking through all discipline, and utterly unmindful of the cries of the enraged O'Kane, the rebels faced about and ran for the woods. A loud huzza from the fort accompanied this exhibition of cowardice. O'Kane was compelled to follow his men; and as they came to a halt just in the edge of the forest, he again urged them to an attack on the fort. But they steadily refused to advance an inch. They had experienced bad usage in their former attempts, and were not at all inclined to test again the mettle of their loyal opponents. Finding all attempts to induce them to make another trial of no avail, O'Kane sullenly gave them orders to march, which they obeyed with alacrity. They did not take up their former line of march, however, but continued up the river, leaving their dead and wounded to be cared for by the Unionists.

The Unionists, who were greatly inferior in numbers, did not feel inclined to risk what they had gained by following, and they were permitted to depart in peace.

While Marvin was at the Settlement, where he had fought so bravely in the defence of the lives and property of others, he little dreamed of the scenes that were enacting near his own humble home.

A detachment of O'Kane's Guard started early in the evening, on the day subsequent to the scenes which we have been relating, bent upon the capture of Captain Wilson and Archie Carter. The expedition was composed of one hundred and eighty men, including O'Kane and his Aid, provided with boats of almost every description, and fully armed and accoutred for the formidable undertaking of arresting two men. With the utmost possible caution and silence they proceeded down the river to the spot designated, where the men were landed and the boats secreted. They waited at this place in silence, sitting within the shade of the forest to escape observation, until nearly eleven o'clock, when they started in the direction of the cabin.

When they had arrived within a quarter of a mile of the destined spot, the main body was brought to a dead halt, and O'Kane and one of his sergeants moved cautiously forward to reconnoitre. They found the cabin all dark, while perfect silence reigned without and within. One thing, however, perplexed O'Kane. He doubted not that Wilson and Archie were slumbering within. He had supposed that Captain Wilson's company at Clay's Settlement was under command of Lieutenant Rollins. Still he thought it possible they might be in the neighborhood of their captain. Feeling secure, however, in the consciousness of superior numbers, he returned to his comrades, determined to push on and secure his prey, at all hazards.

The Guards cautiously approached, headed by O'Kane, who was armed with an axe. They arrived in front of the cabin undisturbed, and then completely encircled it, in order to prevent the possibility of an escape. A few heavy blows from O'Kane's axe demolished the door, and he rushed in with his weapon uplifted, shouting, at the top of his voice, —

"I command you to surrender, in the name of the Confederate States of America."

He paused for an answer; but none came.

"It is useless to think of escape," he continued, "for you are entirely surrounded, and your only hope for mercy lies in your immediate surrender!"

Still no reply came to his pompous declaration, and he ordered one of his men to strike a light. This was quickly accomplished, and the mortified O'Kane found that the cabin was without an inmate. He stood for some time, not attempting to conceal his chagrin; and then he shouted to his men, —

"Let us burn the wigwam; they may be concealed in it!"

A large quantity of dry brush was soon placed upon the floor of the cabin, and the torch applied. As the logs of which it was composed were dry, it was soon completely wrapped in flame. The rebels stood around it in a circle, eagerly expecting the appearance of Wilson and Archie. But, alas for their loyalty to the Confederate government, they came not.

The rebels waited until the last flickering flame of the burning building had expired, and the forest was again overshadowed with darkness, ere they gave up all hope of securing the objects of their search; but then they were compelled to give up, and their crestfallen captain gave orders for a homeward march. They soon came up to their boats; and, ere the day had dawned, the Guards had returned, perfectly bloodless, and were most of them in a sound slumber.

O'Kane chafed furiously under his disappointment, and sought his couch, breathing forth vows of vengeance, "loud and deep." He had hoped to secure Wilson, whom above all other men he dreaded. He knew of his attachment to his niece, of his prompt and daring character, and he feared lest he might prove a troublesome obstacle in the way of the final and successful accomplishment of some of his plans.

CHAPTER X.

CAPTAIN WILSON remained here with his men until the middle of September. Price and his army were at Springfield, and it was supposed he had gone into winter quarters. The inhabitants of the Settlement prevailed upon Captain Wilson to remain with them a little while longer. While here, Marvin had learned from a woman that Cora was not dead, but had been removed to some distant locality in the southern part of the state, by the direction of O'Kane. Marvin's heart leaped with joy at the information of the woman in regard to Cora.

Marvin went immediately to Archie, and informed him what the woman had told him about Cora. Archie said to Marvin, —

"As it is only a few miles up the river to O'Kane's house, I'm a good mind to take the skiff and go and see what the old porcupine is about up there."

"That excursion would be attended with some danger," said Marvin. "You know very well that as long as Price remains in Springfield O'Kane and his guard will be ransacking this section of the country."

"That mought all be," said Archie. "I've got tired of lounging around here."

"We are doing our duty," said Marvin, "in protecting the people from the assaults of the rebel banditti."

"Wal," said Archie, "I shall go. I shan't be reconciled with myself until I hear what the old critter has to say about Cora, anyhow."

In a few moments Archie had floated his skiff into the river, and then he rowed towards O'Kane's. When within a few rods of the house, Archie secreted the skiff, and looked cautiously around to ascertain if any one was stirring. Finding that all was quiet, he marched boldly up to the house, and, without knocking, entered the kitchen. Rebecca was standing at a table, with her back towards him, when he entered, and ere she turned round he had coolly seated himself in a chair. When Rebecca saw that Archie Carter was in her presence, she was perfectly thunderstruck. Her eyes enlarged to twice their natural dimensions, and the end of her sharp nose turned as white as chalk.

"Don't blush so, ma'am," said Archie, with a smile that stretched his huge mouth from ear to ear, at the same time placing his hand upon his heart. "I raally couldn't bear to leave the country forever without seein' on ye once more. The fact is, ma'am," said he, bowing very low, "I do love you awfully, though I say it myself; and you might travel many a mile and not find as likely a lookin' man as what I am myself."

Whilst Archie was delivering himself of this gallant speech, Miss Rebecca had somewhat recovered her mental equilibrium. By the time that Archie brought his passionate declamation to a close, her tongue had become loosened on its pivot.

"What are you doing here, you great rascal that you are? What are you doing here again?" she exclaimed furiously.

"Don't blame me at all, ma'am," said Archie, smiling; "don't blame *me*, ma'am. It's your beautiful face that's did the hull. I should had to come back if the devil forbid me."

Rebecca was fairly stumped. The cool impudence of Archie was more than she could quickly decide how to handle; but she finally exclaimed,—

"What do you mean, you lying vagabond?"

"I don't wonder you think I lie, ma'am, when I call you handsome," replied Archie; "but all folks don't see alike at all. You've smit my gizzard, ma'am, and no mistake!"

"Ain't you ashamed, you great villain, to insult a virtuous female in this manner, when you see she is all alone?" cried Rebecca.

"Ma'am, now don't say so!" said Archie, beseechingly; "now don't accuse me of sich ongenteel conduct. Only let me kiss you once, ma'am, and you'll find that I am sincere in my pretensions."

"O Lord!" screamed Rebecca, elevating both hands, and rolling her eyes upwards. "You talk of kissing me, do you, you old scoundrel! You just try that once," she continued, lowering her hands, and extending her fingers like hawks' claws, "you try that once, and I'll scratch your eyes out, you brute!"

"O, dear!" sighed Archie, "you've ondid me, ma'am — clear ondid me. You've conspired me with a vi'lent passion, and now you refuse me only one kiss. O, ma'am, you're too cruel!"

"Get out of my house, you impudent villain!" screeched the virago; "get out of my house! O, if the servants were only here, or O'Kane! they'd give you your deserts, you great bear!"

"Ma'am," said Archie, with a rueful visage, "I've come a great distance to see you; and if you won't accept the offer of my heart, I hope you'll be generous enough to give me a bit of luncheon."

"You don't eat a bit in this house, you low-bred marauder!" exclaimed Rebecca. "You've eat here once too often, now. So, begone with yourself this moment!"

"Look here, you old dromedary," said Archie, suddenly altering his tone; "get me something to eat, or, blow me, I'll cut out your tongue for you!"

Rebecca seeming not inclined to obey, Archie thundered again in her ear,—

"Get me something to eat, you old shark; for I must be off. Don't make me speak agin!"

9

"I won't, so there, if I die for it," said Rebecca, snappishly.

"Then, my dear, I'll get it myself," said Archie, rising from his chair, and approaching a cupboard which was standing in one corner of the room. "You ain't generous at all, ma'am," said he, opening the door, and drawing forth two large pies, and coolly depositing them under his arm. Turning to Rebecca, he said, —

"Old damsel, you must be pretty well acquainted with me by this time. You know, I guess, that I generally do about as I promise. Now, harkee: I don't war with she folks, no way; but I want to ax you one question; and if you don't make a correct answer, I'll choke your old weasand for you. Where's O'Kane's niece?"

Rebecca, turning pale, replied, —

"She is not dead, but has been removed to the southern part of the state; and that's all I know about it."

Archie, seeing that he could worm no more out of the old virago, left the house, and started with all speed towards the skiff. When he arrived there, it was about noon; and seating himself beneath a tree, he partook hastily of one of Rebecca's pies, and then proceeded down the river towards the Settlement. He labored faithfully at the oars, and shortly after four o'clock entered the village. Archie went directly to Captain Wilson, and told him that he had not been able to get any additional news in regard to the whereabouts of Cora. Captain Wilson detailed part of his men to assist the settlers in putting the fort in perfect repair, so that they would feel secure against another attack from O'Kane, and then concluded to return to the army. The next morning, they bade adieu to their friends, and in two days reached the headquarters of General Sigel.

CHAPTER XI.

KIND reader, we will now return to Cora, whom we left some time since in her desolate situation. The evening after the conversation she had heard, Cora retired to her bed with the determination to stay in the house no longer. "But where shall I go?" she asked herself. "I cannot return to my uncle's, and I have no one to protect me;" and the tears flowed down her cheeks as they had a thousand times before. While her heart was filled with sadness, there was one ray of light flitted across her mind: she remembered well what the man had said, that the Union army would soon be there. "Now," she said to herself, "if I can only contrive to make my escape from the custody of the old woman, and get within the lines of the Union army, if I do not meet with Marvin, I shall at least be with friends." She then determined to try all possible ways to make her escape. "If I die in the attempt, it can be no worse for me; for the treatment I receive here is almost beyond endurance." The next morning she arose more refreshed than she had been for many mornings previous. "Now," she said to herself, "I must watch every opportunity to make my escape."

Cora, up to this time, had been closely watched by the old woman; yet once or twice she had been allowed the privilege of going into the old woman's room, which adjoined hers. It was nearly eight o'clock when she came in with Cora's coarse breakfast. Cora observed that she looked deadly pale, and could but just walk.

"Well, miss," said she, "I have had a mighty bad night of it, and I am sick now;" and as she turned to go out of the room, she fell to the floor in a fit. Cora, seeing her in this state, was at first terribly frightened; but in a moment she regained her self-possession, and ran for some water, with which she bathed the old woman's head, which so revived her, that, with Cora's help, she managed to get to her bed. Cora, in all the tenderness of her heart, prepared for her some herb tea, which quickly relieved her pain, and soothed her to sleep; and as she had had no rest during the night, her sleep now became sound. Cora now found herself, at least for a moment, at liberty; and she was determined, although that was not the time to make her escape, to prepare for it. She turned around and looked at the old woman, who was still sleeping soundly. She then went to the door, and looked out, as she had not had that privilege before since she had been there. As she came back into the room, she discovered an old reticule lying upon the floor. She had the curiosity to examine it, and, to her great delight, found the key to her trunk. She again looked at the old woman, who had turned over in bed, and was still sleeping. She found her trunk under the bed. She now moved it carefully out, opened it, and selected from her clothing a calico dress, a thin shawl, and a Shaker bonnet. She carried them out and hid them under some brush, a few steps from the house.

After she had accomplished all this, which she did in less time than it takes us to record it, she returned to the bed, and was in the act of bathing the old woman's temple, when she awoke somewhat refreshed. Cora asked her if she should go back to her room. The old woman made an effort to rise, but she was so weak she could not. She told Cora she might remain with her until the old man came back from town.

In a little while the old man came in, and was somewhat surprised to find the old woman worse, and Cora nursing her. The old woman had just strength enough to tell him what a poor time she had had, and that she would have died had it not been for Cora. .

"Wal," said the old man, "I thought the gal was mighty nice, when she first come here; and that it was a cussed mean trick to shut her up here against her will, and keep her so long. But you see, gal," turning to Cora, that the old woman was going to make a great heap out of it, and I lets her have her own way. But, old woman," said he, "Bill White told me to-day that Martin was at Cairo, and that Lincoln's army was around there, and if he should get gobbled up, you would never get any pay for the gal's staying here. I tell you, old critter, Martin has euchred you; and I shouldn't care if she toted off this very day."

The old woman sank back on her pillow, and closed her eyes. The conversation of the old man somewhat surprised Cora, and it led her to believe that he would have no objection to her leaving.

All the afternoon the old-woman was very sick, and Cora had to remain with her. She retired to her room that night, and the old man took her place as nurse. The next morning she found the old woman not much better.

At breakfast, the old man told Cora that Bill White was a kind of partner of Martin's; and, he said, "If he knew the old woman was sick, he would come and carry you off. Now, if you want to return to your friends, you may go to-morrow morning; and I will show you a path by which you can go, and not go near the town."

Cora expressed to him her heartfelt thanks, and promised to reward him if it ever lay in her power.

Cora was up the next morning before the sun. The old man had gone to the spring for some water; and, while he was gone, she slipped out and brought in her clothing that she had hid in the brush. She was not long in preparing breakfast, and when the old man came in they sat down.

After breakfast the old man told her to prepare for her journey. She went into her room and changed her clothing; then came out and tied up a few things that she found in her trunk. In a short time she was ready to start.

The old man led her to the path she was to take. "Now," said he, "gal, you keep this path; do not turn to the right or left, but keep right straight ahead. And may God bless you."

Cora thanked him, and added, if she was so fortunate as to reach her friends, she would remember this act of kindness.

Cora made good progress, issuing from the ten-mile wood about eleven o'clock. She had followed the sandy cart path which led through it. The pine barrens, being almost destitute of under-wood and flowers, had great monotony. Mile after mile it was the same dull level.

When she reached the open country, the sun poured down its fur-nace heat, and her feet were sore with the hot sand. But she was willing to suffer hardships to get out of the power of her uncle. While stopping here a moment to rest, a slave rode up, with a mule team, drawing a small load of wood.

"Why, he!" said he; "who's runnin' off now?"

Cora looked up, in surprise, at the bright-looking, good-natured negro of twenty.

"I begs your pardon, miss; you kep' your head down, an' I said to myse'f, 'Pears like dish sher is some poor slave woman, an' I'll jist give her a lift an' let her ride a piece; but, as you is a poor white, you is jist as welcome to a seat in my wagon."

Cora made no reply to what the slave had said, and gladly took a seat beside him.

"Where are you going?" he asked.

This was a serious and a fearful question. Her only thought was to get to her Union friends. The direct way to go she did not know, nor the names of the towns she should pass through. Waiv-ing the question, she asked the slave if he knew the name of the next town.

"It is Cass, miss; and it is a right smart of a journey; it will take two or three days for you to walk there. But I will whip up my mules, and tote you a piece of the way. Massa will not know, 'case, you see, massa has gone to de war."

"Do you know anything about the war?" asked Cora.

"Well, some," replied the slave; "the Union army was coming, massa said, the other day."

"Do you know any one in Cass?" asked Cora.

"Well, I have been there for massa; but I don't know any white folks there. If you will wait until I unload this wood, I will tote you a good ways towards there; and here is some lunch in my basket."

The slave proceeded to give Cora some cold turkey and plum pudding, which he obtained from the cook, a particular friend of his, being the remnants of yesterday's dinner of the family. Cora sat down and ate some, while the slave unloaded his wood. Very soon he came back, and said, —

"I will tote you a piece farther now; massa is gone, and I'm boss now; and I think that I can take you to a cabin, where lives an old man, about four miles from here, and the old man will keep you over night. He is a Moravian preacher."

Cora felt that if she could only get there, he might be her friend. It was past sundown when Cora arrived at the cabin of the preacher. The old man, with his long, flowing, white beard, was sitting at his cabin door when Cora came up.

"Good evening," said the old man as Cora approached him, with an expression of kindness on his countenance that bespoke that she had met with a friend indeed.

"Good evening," replied Cora. "Could I have the privilege of remaining here to-night, as I have travelled a long way to-day?" asked Cora.

"You can," said the old man. "My home is a humble one, and my fare coarse, but such as it is, I am willing to share it with you. Walk in, miss."

Cora entered the cabin. The old man had but a few articles of furniture; but they were very neatly arranged about the room. On a shelf, fastened up with cords, lay the old Bible. After they had finished their evening meal, the old man turned to Cora, and asked where she was going.

"Friend," said Cora, "my journey is long, and my story is a sad one; and, while the dark clouds of war are hovering over us, — and such a war as this, where brother is arrayed against brother, and neighbor against neighbor, — a poor fugitive, escaping from the cruelties of those that would deprive her of that which was dear in this life, and even life itself, and all for the possession of that patrimony that her dead father desired that she should receive and enjoy, must first know that she is with a true friend."

The old man said that he was the friend of the bowed down and the distressed, and she could place the most implicit confidence in him, and if he could ameliorate her condition, he would willingly do it.

Cora now commenced the sorrowful story. It was late at night when she lay down in a corner of the room upon a bed of wild beasts' skins, which the old man had prepared for her. Being very tired, and feeling perfectly secure, she was soon asleep.

The old man had been up some time before Cora awoke in the morning, and she found him preparing a breakfast for them. After they had eaten, Cora made preparations to leave, although her feet were very sore. The old man desired her to stay a few days, but she was afraid to; she thought she was too near Martin's friends to make a long stop.

"Well," said the old man, "it is a long way to the Union lines, and there are a great many bands of guerrillas around here. It is quite a number of miles to Cass, and I do not think you could get there to-night. I will go with you to a house some seven miles from here, on your way, where the people are very kind, and will take care of you over night."

The old man now got ready to accompany Cora; and, as they walked steadily along, she thought of the troubles that were past, and what she must still endure, but she was willing to put her trust in God, and hope for the best.

It was nearly eleven o'clock when the old man and Cora arrived at the house of the old man's friends.

"Well," said the old man to the woman of the house, "is Mr. Fobbs at home?"

She replied that he was, and would be in soon. The old man then told the woman that this young lady felt desirous to reach that part of the state where the Union army was.

While they were conversing, Mr. Fobbs came in, and joined in the conversation. He said that this section of the country·was overrun with bands of rebel soldiers; that they were riding around, and it would be almost impossible for Cora to go in safety. "So I think she had better remain here, until we provide a way for her. I don't feel myself safe here. Colonel Thompson, 'the swamp fox,' is picking up all the men he can find, and I am determined not to enter the rebel ranks. And, as I can't remain here long in safety, I've made up my mind to start this very night for Houston, and I will carry the girl within a couple of miles of Springfield."

At dark, Fobbs drove to the door, and in a few moments they were on the road. The cart was not so easy a vehicle as Cora had rode in before, but it was preferable to going on foot.

The next morning they were within a few miles of Springfield. Here Mr. Fobbs told Cora that he must leave her, as he did not deem it safe for him to enter the town.

Cora felt happy that she had arrived so far towards her journey's end; but yet she felt that if she could find a friend here, to direct her the way she should go, it would be fortunate. As she was walking up the street, she was accosted by a man wearing the Confederate uniform, who asked her where she was going.

"To see my friends," replied Cora, walking on. At this moment he grasped her by the arm, and said, —

"Hold on here! You are going to be free on the strength of Fremont's Proclamation, are you?"

Cora saw at once that she was in trouble. What to do she did not know. As the man held her by the arm, tears flowed down her cheeks; but she said nothing.

"Now," said the man, "you must tell me where you are going."

"To my friends," replied Cora.

"Where are your friends?" he inquired.

"I will not tell you," said Cora.

"You're a runaway, I reckon. We've a safe place for all such as you are."

The man now led Cora before the justice of the town; and, as they were going along, the crowd cried out, —

"What's the row?"

"Why," replied the man, "this girl has strayed into town, and can give no reasonable account of herself. She wants to see her friends; and I am taking her to the justice."

When they arrived at the justice's office, the justice asked the man, "Who have you there?"

"A runaway slave," said the soldier.

"She is no slave, or nigger," said Mrs. Johnson, the jailer's wife, who stood in the door; "she is white as I am."

" That may be," said the justice; " we have white slaves as well as black ones, and if she is at all suspected of being a runaway, we must commit her to jail — the receptacle of criminals and slaves."

This was a trying time to Cora. What could she do? She did not dare to tell who her friends were; and if her uncle should find her out, then it would be worse for her.

It was past twelve o'clock when she entered the jail, and, as she was very sad and weary, she did not fully realize her condition; so she sank down to rest.

In a few minutes the jailer entered, and asked her a few questions. Cora replied that she should answer no questions; that she was no slave.

" Well, miss, I don't think that you are; but I must obey orders. I am willing to make you as comfortable as possible."

He now went out; but returned in a few minutes with a husk mattress and bed clothing, and also something to eat.

" Here, miss," said he, " make yourself as comfortable as you can."

After the jailer went out, Cora sat upon the bed, and a sigh escaped her lips. Here she was, deprived of liberty, friends, and all the comforts of life.

" O," she exclaimed, " what would my poor dead father say, if he only knew what his darling child suffered ! When all his faculties were employed in the accumulation of wealth, that his daughter might enjoy it, little did he think she would ever suffer such terrible trials at the hands of her nearest relatives."

She thought of Marvin. If he only knew her condition and situation, he would leave everything, and dare all, and fly upon the wings of love and release her.

For two long days no one visited her in her prison home. Within a few rods of the jail lived a colored woman, named Parker. She had been a slave, but had been liberated by her master, who left her a little property. She had always detested the jail, yet she was a frequent visitor to ameliorate the condition of such of her race as were so unfortunate as to be imprisoned there. On the third day of Cora's imprisonment the good woman came in, and as the jailer had spoken to her in regard to Cora, she had a great desire to see her. The jailer said he was willing to give her the opportunity, and would lead her to Cora's cell. When she entered,

10

Cora was seated upon her bed, with both her hands covering her face, sobbing bitterly.

"Miss," said the old colored woman, kindly, "will you tell me who you are?"

"I am no slave."

"I know that," said the old woman. And she spoke in such kind tones that Cora took courage.

"I am no slave, and I do *so* want to leave this horrid place."

"I will see what I can do for you, my dear."

The good woman now went to see the jailer, to know what could be done in gaining Cora's liberty. The jailer said *he* was willing Cora should go, but he supposed she must be sold for the justice's fees, and the expense he had been to in keeping her in jail; and, before he could release her, he must have an order from the justice. He went directly to the justice's office, who made out a bill for his fee, and an order for the girl's release. This done, he carried it, in connection with his own bill, to the colored woman, who immediately paid the whole.

"Now," said the jailer, "you can take the girl home, as your slave."

She now went with the jailer into Cora's cell. As soon as Cora saw her, she came towards her, and said, —

"My friend, can you do anything for me?"

"I have," replied the colored woman. "You can now go with me. Although against my conscience, I had to buy you, in order to get you out."

"O, God!" cried Cora, "am I a slave? O, Infinite Wisdom, when will my cup of misery be full? Is it now, and have I drank it to the dregs?"

Mrs. Parker told the jailer that she was no poor white, or slave, but a lady, "and I know it," she said.

"I think so myself," replied the jailer; "and I'm afraid we shall all have to suffer for this, sooner or later."

The colored woman now led Cora out of the jail, soothing her as best she could as they walked along.

"O," said Cora, "I thank you a thousand times; but I have not the money to pay you for what you have already done."

"That is a matter we will talk about when your mind is a little more reconciled than it is to-day."

Cora had been with the colored woman about a week, when she told the woman who she was and where she intended to go. Mrs. Parker told her that she had yet some distance to go, and that she had better remain with her a while longer, which Cora agreed to do. That very afternoon, Mr. Fobbs came in, and, in conversation with Mrs. Parker, told her that he was going to join the Federal army at Rolla. In reply to Mrs. Parker's suggestion that Cora should accompany him to the Federal lines, he thought it would not be proper. At this moment he heard the sound of a trumpet, and, looking out, saw a company of rebel cavalry coming towards the house. He turned to Mrs. Parker, and said, " This will be a pretty hot place for me soon, so I must bid you good by."

CHAPTER XII.

In a few days after Captain Wilson reported to General Sigel, he was ordered to hold himself in readiness for duty at any moment. As Archie was sitting by the side of Marvin one evening, in their tent, he broke the silence by exclaiming, —

" I reckon O'Kane will have to suffer for all of this yet. But, blame me ! I regret one thing."

" What is that ? " asked Marvin.

" I regret that I did not kiss the old porcupine the time I took her pies."

" Well, you may have that privilege yet," said Marvin.

" You are joking, now, captain, and I know it. But if I ever get a good sight at O'Kane, he never will know what hurt him, I reckon. He is doomed ; and if there is any truth in preaching, he can't prosper. The way he has treated his niece is enough to condemn any man."

" Yes," said Marvin, " there is a just God that rules, and to him he must look for mercy. I have not mentioned Cora's name to you since we were at the Settlement ; but I have thought of her, and have sworn before high Heaven to avenge her wrongs."

At this point of the conversation, Lieutenant Rollins entered the tent, having posted the guard for the night, as it was nearly sundown. The three officers had just seated themselves for their evening meal, when an orderly brought an order to Captain Wilson,

requesting his presence at headquarters. Captain Wilson did not
stop to finish his meal, but hastened there immediately. As he
entered, General Sigel said, —

"Captain, here is a man that has come in from the rebel lines.
He says that there has been an intelligent young lady sold into
slavery; that her family resided somewhere about Osceola; and
that her name is Cora O'Kane. Now, captain, have you ever
known such a young lady?"

Marvin turned pale at this information, and answered him in the
affirmative. He related to the general how her uncle abducted her
from home, and carried her off to parts unknown, that he might
retain the property bequeathed to her by her father. The general
ordered Marvin to retire to his quarters, and make preparations to
march to her rescue on the following day. As soon as Marvin had
returned to his tent, he sought Archie, and related to him what had
transpired at headquarters.

"Now, Archie, are you ready for the undertaking?" said Marvin.

"I am with you, Marvin, by the roaring Jehu!" exclaimed Archie; "and I'll be cussed if I won't chew them all into shoe-strings,
but what we will have that ar gal yet."

"Well, Archie," said Marvin, "I am glad you are with me in
this undertaking."

They now retired for the night; but Marvin could not sleep for
the thought of meeting Cora again, and perhaps finally uniting his
destiny to hers. A new existence seemed to dawn upon him. His
feelings were tumultuous; yet they were mingled now and then
with a fear that it might all prove in the end an illusion.

The next morning, Marvin rose early, and began making preparations for their departure. At ten o'clock, Lieutenants Carter and
Rollins had formed the men in line, ready to march. Captain
Wilson now rode up in front of his men, and addressed them as
follows : —

"Comrades, we are about to start upon an expedition that will
require every man to keep a strict lookout; and it is my wish that
each man do his duty promptly and efficiently, so that, when I return, I shall be able to give a good report of every one of you."

After Captain Wilson had closed his remarks to his men, they
gave three hearty cheers, and rode from camp. In the afternoon
of the third day from camp, as Archie was riding some little ways

in front of the company, he discovered a rebel trail. He immediately wheeled, and ordered the company to halt; then riding up to Captain Wilson, he said, —

"These infernal secesh are about here, and no mistake! Now, I think we had better camp here; and I will jump off my horse, and follow the trail, and see what I can find."

Archie, as good as his word, dismounted, and took the trail that led into the forest. Captain Wilson ordered his men to dismount, and prepare to camp. Archie moved cautiously along on the trail for about two miles down the river, until he came to a little opening. There he discovered an encampment of rebels. It was a spot so little exposed to discovery, that the band had thrown off the restraints of war. They had no pickets out, and their horses were loose, browsing on the luxuriant foliage. The fires for cooking their supper were burning in the bright glow of sunset. Some of the men were cooking, some eating, and others lounged upon the grass in front of their tents, playing cards.

Archie, crawling down among the bushes, got so near that he could almost hear them converse. He was satisfied that it was O'Kane and his Guard. He cautiously returned to camp, and told Captain Wilson that they had struck the trail of O'Kane, "and a pretty set of cut-throats they are too," said he. Archie proposed to the captain that they should leave their horses where they were, and march as carefully as they could, and take the camp by surprise. Captain Wilson assented to this proposal, and ordered his men to secure the horses to the trees, and prepare to march.

"Don't lose half of the victory," said Archie, "by being in too big a hurry. Let us rest ourselves, and eat something, and then be ready for work."

The most of them obeyed the injunction, catching a brief sleep while they waited for orders. Some three or four of the company could neither eat nor sleep. Obscured in its own shadow, the dense forest was soon enveloped in darkness, and they waited patiently for the rising of the full harvest moon in the east. A more favorable hour for the attacking party could not have been desired. They were enabled to steal into the very camp of the enemy before they were discovered. Silent and fierce as the tiger whose young has been stolen from her, they pressed up to the very tent doors.

"Who goes there?" cried out suddenly a sharp-eared bandit.

His answer was a bullet through the heart. Of the whole camp which sprang to find the cause of the alarm, twenty bit the dust at the first fire. The men, surprised, and some of them at a distance from their arms, could hardly distinguish in the moonlight friend from foe; but the Unionists had marked them, and bore them down resistlessly. O'Kane's men now fought desperately. Those that lost their rifles drew their knives, with which they made a stout resistance. On rushed Captain Wilson towards the tent, which, by a small, dark flag flying near it, and its superior size, was marked as that of O'Kane. Coming to the door, with rifle in hand and sword at his side, he looked out for the cause of the *mêlée*. The moon shone full upon his figure and dark face. It was O'Kane, and Marvin Wilson stood before him. One flash of those glowing eyes told him how matters stood. For a moment he stood amazed, then, with a deadly spring, rushed at the avenger, and fired, but missed the object of his fierce hate. He now ran in circles, and doubled, to escape the aim of his enemies; but he was the object of too righteous a wrath to escape the onset of the resolute men who pressed upon him. He fell, pierced by half a dozen bullets. Rising upon his elbow, he drew his revolver, and aimed at his nearest foe; and the chance shot of his dying hand pierced the arm of Marvin.

"Take that, you sneaking, prowling wolf!" yelled Archie in the ear of the expiring man. "That's for burning our captain's cabin, and your base treatment of your niece," and he plunged his bowie-knife through the body of O'Kane. "I have kept my oath, and I am satisfied."

The remainder of the band, seeing the fall of their leader, took to flight, catching their horses as they could, and making for the woods; but they were met by Lieutenant Rollins and a portion of the men, who gave them such a volley that but few escaped. It was not until Archie turned from the corpse of O'Kane, that he discovered that Marvin was wounded. He immediately ran to him, and inquired if he was badly hurt.

"I think not," said Archie; "it is only a flesh wound in the arm."

One of the men brought a lighted torch to Archie, who closely examined the wound.

"It's nothing but a scratch," said Archie, "and a little plaster will fix that all right."

Archie suggested that Marvin had better be removed to O'Kane's tent for the night.

" I can easily walk there myself," said Marvin, which he did.

Archie ordered the tent to be guarded, while he 'and some of the men went back to look after their horses. Finding them all right, they concluded to take them to the late rebel encampment, and there remain until morning. The men now went to work and re-kindled the smouldering fires of the rebels, and prepared themselves some refreshments. Archie, in the capacity of surgeon, was busily at his sad work, while the men were bringing the wounded together. And thus they worried out the night.

In the morning, Marvin beheld the corpse of O'Kane. He was stretched out at full length upon the ground in his uniform of the Confederate Guard. A hideous grin distorted his features, and he appeared to have left the world in great agony. After the men had buried the dead, Captain Wilson and his officers held a council, to ascertain what they had better do, as they found that four of their own men were wounded, and about twenty of O'Kane's Guard. They proposed to go no farther at present, but to return with their wounded, who must receive immediate relief. Archie ordered his men to make preparations for carrying the wounded. They managed to fit up three of O'Kane's wagons for that purpose. When the men had appropriated all the valuables which they could find to their own use, they set fire to the encampment, and left.

When Marvin's men had put the wounded rebels into the wagon, they found Lieutenant Colonel Rice, of O'Kane's Guard, badly wounded; and, in conversation with Captain Wilson, he told him that O'Kane had been in camp, where he was surprised, about three days, and that they were on their way to join Price. As O'Kane was determined to do but little fighting outside of Missouri, he had been in no hurry about moving.

CHAPTER XIII.

THEY had not gone a great distance on their way back before they were happily surprised by meeting Majors Zagonyi and White, with their commands, on their way to Springfield. Captain Wilson told them that he had just had a fight with O'Kane, and had anni-

hilated his Guard, and he was now on his return with the wounded
to Rolla; and he proposed, after conversing with them a while as to
the route they should take to Springfield, to detach a squad of men,
in charge of a sergeant, to take the wounded to Rolla, while he and
the rest of his men accompanied Zagonyi to Springfield. They
were soon on their way, and, by marching all night, arrived at
Springfield early next morning. As they had made a detour of
twelve miles, this brought them to the right of the town.

On reaching the outskirts of Springfield, they found twelve hundred infantry and four hundred cavalry were posted on the crown
of a hill, prepared for and awaiting them. But the brave Unionists
did not quail. A miry brook and a stout rail fence, where sharpshooters were judiciously posted behind the trees and fences, were
the first things the Unionists discovered as they approached the enemy. They could see no entrance but through a very narrow lane.
Zagonyi advanced to Captain Wilson, and handed him the glass;
who looked through it towards the enemy.

"You observe, captain," said the major, "the obstacles to be
overcome before we can get very near the rebels. That fence must
be taken down, and those sharpshooters silenced, before we can
strike. Can you accomplish that work, captain?"

"I will try," said Captain Wilson; and he turned to his brave
comrades, and said, —

"My lads, we have an important work to perform. Be steady,
be vigilant, and fight with your usual bravery."

Marvin now divided his men into two platoons, he commanding
one and Archie the other. Captain Wilson now gave the word
of command: —

"By the right flank, march!" and they rushed to their work.
All this was the act of a moment; but when that moment had
passed, seventy of Marvin's men, dead and wounded, were stretched
upon the ground. This caused Marvin to be more frantic, and he
rushed on to the enemy with the fury of a lion. Archie's voice was
heard above the din of battle. Zagonyi, closely watching the movements of Marvin, turned to his brave guard, and said, —

"Now is the time, boys! Come on — I will lead you! Let the
watchword be, 'The Union and Fremont!' Draw sabres! Quick
step, march!"

Up to this time no guardsman has struck a blow. Their time

has come. Lieutenant Mathenyi, with thirty men, is ordered to attack the cavalry. With sabres flashing over their heads, the little band of heroes spring towards their tremendous foe. Right upon the centre they charge. The dense mass opens, the blue-coats force their way in, and the whole rebel squadron scatter in disgraceful flight through the cornfields in the rear. The boys follow them, sabring the fugitives. Days afterwards, the enemy's horse lie thick among the uncut corn. Zagonyi holds his main body until Maythenyi disappears in the cloud of rebel cavalry; then his voice rises through the air, —

"In open order — charge!"

The line opens out, to give play to their sword-arm. Steeds respond to the order of their riders, and, quick as thought, with thrilling cheers, the noble hearts rush into the leaden torrent which pours down the incline. With unabated fire, the gallant fellows press through. The fierce onset is not even checked. The foe do not wait for them — they waver, break, and fly. The guardsmen spur into the midst of the rout, and their fast-falling swords work a terrible revenge. Some of the boldest of the Southrons retreat into the woods, and continue a murderous fire from behind trees and thickets. Seven guard-horses fall upon a space not more than twenty feet square. As his steed sinks under him, one of the officers is caught around the shoulders by a grape-vine, and hangs dangling in the air until he is cut down by his friends. The rebel foot are flying in furious haste from the field. Some take refuge in the fair-ground; some hurry into the cornfields; but the greater part run along the edge of the wood, swarm over the fence into the road, and hasten to the village. The guardsmen follow. Zagonyi leads them. Over the loudest roar of battle rings his clarion voice: —

"Come on, Old Kentuck! I'm with you!" and the flash of his sword-blade tells his men where to go.

As he approaches a barn, a man steps from behind the door and lowers his rifle; but, before it has reached a level, Zagonyi's sabre-point descends upon his head, and his life-blood leaps to the very top of the huge barn door. The conflict now rages through the village — in the public square and along the streets. Up and down the guards ride in squads of three or four, and, wherever they see a group of the enemy, charge upon and scatter them. It is hand

11

to hand. No one but has a share in the fray. After the rebels had been driven from their works, they rushed for the village, and Captain Wilson and Archie, with their little command, followed them. Marvin's horse stumbled and fell, and, while he was trying to extricate himself from the fallen steed, he severely injured his wounded arm. A colored woman, seeing the dilemma the Union officer was placed in, rushed out of her house to his rescue. At this moment, Archie turned round to see if the captain was near him, and he quickly beheld the plight that he was in. Archie wheeled at once, and went to his assistance, but not until the colored woman had succeeded in getting him up, and was leading him towards her house. Archie secured the captain's horse and his own; and when he entered the colored woman's house, Marvin lay upon the bed, and *Cora* was bathing his head.

As Cora saw Archie enter, she gave him a smile, but spoke not a word, she was so busily engaged in bathing the hero's head. Marvin lay unconscious of what was going on around him. The colored woman now turned to Archie, and said, —

"I do not think he's dangerously injured."

"No, no," said Cora, bending over him. "Speak, Marvin, *do* speak to me."

He smiled as he heard her voice, and opened his eyes. His face was so thin and so pale, that he looked as if months of sickness had passed over him. She now poured between his lips some stimulant. He soon spoke, in a suppressed voice, and said, —

"It's only my arm," which Archie and the woman went about dressing as well as they could. The bustle of preparation for pursuing the enemy now grew so loud, that Archie was obliged to leave, saying, as he turned to go, —

"Captain, I must leave you for a while."

As he entered the street, and seized his horse's rein, to mount, he saw men approaching with Lieutenant Rollins on a stretcher. He was wounded in the thigh, and they were carrying him to the rear.

"Wal," said Archie to himself, "who knows but what my turn will come next?" as he jumped upon his horse, and rode towards the enemy. He had proceeded but a short distance before he saw Zagonyi. He told Archie he should evacuate the town by nightfall. Archie then said, —

"By your permission, major, I will see to the removal of Captain

Wilson immediately; he was severely hurt by the falling of his horse."

"Yes, certainly," said the major. "So brave a hero as he has proved himself must be taken care of."

Lieutenant Archie rode back to Marvin, and preparations were made to remove him from the town; and Cora must certainly go with them. While Archie went to procure a wagon for their conveyance, Marvin amply paid Mrs. Parker for what she had done for Cora and himself. Archie returned in about an hour with a very comfortable vehicle. They were soon on the road, and by sundown had reached a place of safety, and were snugly bivouacked for the night. On the following morning, General Sigel came up with the whole of his command. Captain Wilson remained in this camp three days, where a hospital had been prepared for the reception of the wounded. With the services of a skilful surgeon, and the careful nursing of Cora, Marvin was getting along very well.

While here, Captain Wilson tendered his resignation to General Fremont, which was accepted, as the condition of his arm was such that it would not admit of his performing any actual service for some time. For the heroic bravery of Archie and the men of his command, a furlough of thirty days was accorded.

CHAPTER XIV.

IT was a lovely morning, about the last of September, after the events detailed in the previous chapter, that Captain Wilson and his little band, accompanied by Cora, set out for Clay's Settlement. They proceeded easily along, and did not arrive at the place of destination until the afternoon of the third day of their departure from camp. It had been agreed that they should not halt at the mansion, but proceed at once to the Settlement. When they came within view of the house, Cora was affected to tears, and she wept freely. All around the mansion seemed silent and deserted. There was no one to be seen around the premises, and everything seemed to betoken the absence of the owner.

After Cora had remained three days at the Settlement, she and her friends proceeded to the mansion of which she was now undisputed owner. Rebecca was in great distress at the death of her brother-in-law, and, completely humbled, she implored the forgiveness of Cora, which was readily granted. O'Kane had obtained the fortune of Cora, but, alas for him! only that she might enjoy it. Cora O'Kane was grateful to that Providence that had watched over and defended her amid all the trials she had been called on to pass through. She acknowledged it with gratitude when she thought of her deliverance, and she acknowledged it when she pondered upon the Doom of the Rebel Guard.

On the day after her arrival at the mansion, Cora O'Kane was united to Marvin Wilson by the very minister who had attended him previous to his intended execution, in the presence of Lieutenant Rollins, Archie Carter, and Rebecca. When their furlough had expired, Archie and his men departed to join the army under Sigel. He steadily refused the urgent solicitations of Marvin and his wife to spend his days beneath their roof in ease and plenty.

"I can't," said he. "My country wants my services, Marvin, and she must have 'em. When the war is over, I may take up with your kind offer."

The worthy Archie lived to make good his promise. And now, kind reader, as we have followed Marvin and Cora to a happy union, and the return of Archie to their hospitable roof, here we will leave them, while the whole nation will proclaim, with shouts of joy, WELL DONE, GOOD AND FAITHFUL SOLDIER!

www.ingramcontent.com/pod-product-compliance
Lightning Source LLC
Chambersburg PA
CBHW020313090426
42735CB00009B/1329